and : guide

Munich

architecture & design

Edited and written by Joachim Fischer
Concept by Martin Nicholas Kunz

teNeues

content

to see . culture & education

to see . public

to stay . hotels

to go . eating, drinking, clubbing

to go . wellness, beauty & sport

to shop . mall, retail, showrooms

introduction

Allianz Arena

Bundesgartenschau 2005

München erlebt gegenwärtig eine Art zweite „Gründerzeit" auf dem Gebiet der Architektur. Obwohl durch Geschichte und Tradition geprägt, zieht die Stadt seit einigen Jahren außerdem mit innovativen architektonischen Projekten die Aufmerksamkeit auf sich. In den letzten Jahren erschlossene Großräume wie der ehemalige Flughafen in Riem, innerstädtische Bauprojekte sowie spektakuläre Bauten zur Fußballweltmeisterschaft 2006 und Bundesgartenschau 2005 zeugen von architektonischer Fantasie und Vielseitigkeit. Der *and:guide München* hilft bei der Orientierung über die aktuelle architektonische Entwicklung in München und öffnet darüber hinaus die Augen für verborgene Qualitäten dieser traditionsbewussten und multikulturellen Stadt.

01. **Bürogebäude am Münchner Tor**
Office Block

Allmann Sattler Wappner Architekten

2003
Schenkensdorfstraße 6 + 10
Schwabing

www.allmannsattlerwappner.de

Munich is currently experiencing a period of prosperity like it did at the end of the 19th Century in the field of architecture. While it is influenced by history and tradition, for some years now, the city has also attracted attention because of its innovative architectural projects. During recent years, construction in the greater Munich area ended, such as the former airport site at Riem, inner-city construction projects and the spectacular new structures for the football world championships in 2006 and the federal garden show in 2005, which display architectural fantasy and diversity. The *and: guide Munich* helps you with orientation around Munich's up-to-date architectural development and, more than that, it opens your eyes to hidden qualities of this tradition-conscious and multicultural city.

Fünf Höfe

Neue Messe München

Munich vit actuellement une sorte de deuxième « Gründerzeit » dans le domaine de l'architecture. Bien qu'empreinte de tradition et d'histoire, la ville attire l'attention depuis plusieurs années avec ses projets architectoniques innovants. Les grands espaces architecturaux viabilisés durant les dernières années tels l'ancien aéroport de Riem, ainsi que les projets de construction urbains, les bâtiments spectaculaires dédiés au championat du monde de football 2006 et l'exposition nationale d'horticulture 2005 témoignent de l'imagination architectonique et de sa diversité. Le catalogue *and:guide Munich* permet de se repérer dans le contexte actuel du développement architectural de Munich et révèle les qualités cachées de cette ville multiculturelle et également consciente de ses traditions.

Munich experimenta actualmente una especie de segunda Gründerzeit "época de expansión" en el terreno de la arquitectura. Aunque marcada por la historia y la tradición la ciudad atrae además la atención desde hace algunos años por los proyectos arquitectónicos innovadores. Las grandes áreas urbanizadas en los últimos años como el antiguo aeropuerto en Riem, los proyectos arquitectónicos del centro así como los espectaculares edificios para el Campeonato Mundial de Fútbol de 2006 y la Feria Federal de Jardinería de 2005 dan testimonio de fantasía y variedad arquitectónica. La *and:guide Munich* ayuda a orientarse por el actual desarrollo arquitectónico de Munich abriendo además los ojos para las calidades ocultas de esta ciudad con conciencia de su tradición y multicultural.

HypoVereinsbank

to see . living
office & industry
culture & education
public

Projekt Theresie

KSP Engel und Zimmermann Architekten
OPB Obermeyer Planen + Berater (SE),
CBP Cronauer (SE)

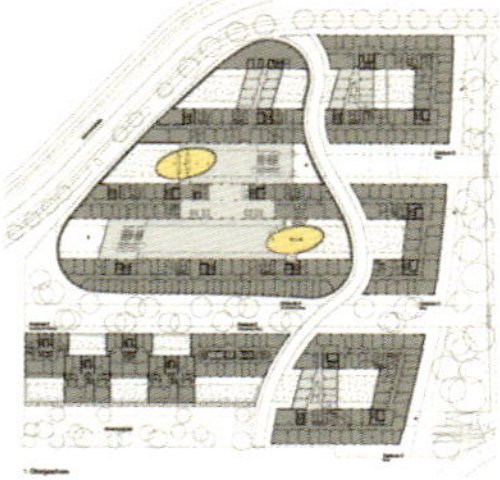

2003
Theresienhöhe 11-13
Schwanthaler Höhe

www.theresie.de
www.ksp-architekten.de

Mit einer lebendigen Mischung aus Alt und Neu, aus Wohnen, Arbeit und Freizeit entsteht hier ein modernes innerstädtisches Wohnquartier. Überdachte Atrien bieten lärm- und wettergeschützte Bereiche, Bürogebäude begrenzen das Gebiet nach Osten, zum Bavariapark im Süden bilden einzeln stehende Wohnhäuser den Abschluss.

With a lively combination of old and new, living, work and freetime, a modern, inner-city residential quarter is developing here. Enclosed atria provide areas, which are sheltered from noise and weather; office blocks define the district's limits towards the east and detached, residential housing marks the end of this zone near Bavariapark in the south.

Combinant l'ancien et le nouveau de manière vivante et mélangeant l'habitat, le travail et les loisirs, il se crée ici un quartier d'habitation urbain au caractère moderne. Des patios recouverts de toits offrent des zones protégées du bruit et des intempéries, le complexe de bureaux limite l'espace vers l'est, des maisons d'habitation séparées orientées au sud vers le Bavariapark clôturent l'espace.

Con una mezcla vivaz de lo nuevo y lo viejo, de la vivienda, el trabajo y el tiempo libre surge aquí un barrio residencial moderno en el centro. Los patios techados ofrecen recintos que protegen del ruido y del clima, los edificios de oficinas limitan el terreno hacia el este, unas viviendas separadas forman el final en el sur hacia el Bavariapark.

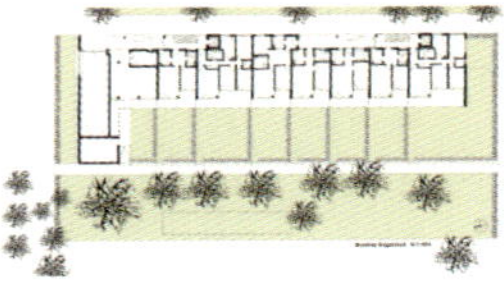

Wohnungsbau am Ackermannbogen

Apartment Construction

Meck Architekten
Ingenieurbüro Haushofer (SE)

2004
Therese-Studer-Straße 17-19
Schwabing

www.meck-architekten.de

Das Gebäude von Prof. Meck spricht eine deutliche architektonische Sprache, die Fassaden spiegeln klar strukturierte Grundrisse wider, Loggien bieten geschützte Freibereiche und erzeugen durch die Vor- und Rücksprünge ein lebendiges Licht- und Schattenspiel.

Prof. Meck's building speaks a straightforward architectural language. The façades reflect clearly structured plans, loggias provide sheltered, open spaces producing a lively play of light and shadows due to the projections and recesses.

Le bâtiment du Prof. Meck a un langage architectonique clair, les façades reflètent les plans bien structurés, les loggias offrent des zones libres protégées et créent des jeux vivants d'ombre et de lumière grâce à des avancées et des retraits.

El edificio del profesor Meck habla un claro lenguaje arquitectónico, las fachadas reflejan plantas claramente estructuradas, las loggias ofrecen recintos libres protegidos y producen una juego vivaz de luces y sombras por medio de entrantes y salientes.

Galeriahaus

Gallery House

Röpke Architekten

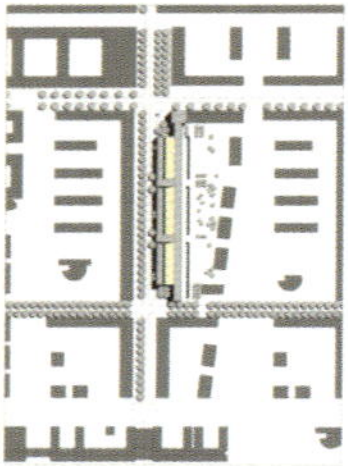

1999
Lehrer-Wirth-Straße 15-19
Messestadt Riem

www.roepkearchitekten.de

Die glasgedeckte Galeria, eine begrünte, lichtdurchflutete Halle, ist nicht nur großzügiger Eingangsbereich für alle 172 Wohnungen. Mit ihren Laubengängen, Treppen, Brücken und Pflanzen vermittelt sie ganzjährig eine offene und kommunikative Atmosphäre.

The gallery with a glass roof, a hallway with green planting and flooded in light is not only a spacious entrance zone for all 172 apartments. The access balconies, stairs, bridges and plants transmit an open and communicative atmosphere all year round.

La galerie au toit de verre et son hall rempli de plantes et baigné de lumière offre plus qu'un espace généreux d'entrée aux 172 appartements. Ses pergolas, ses escaliers, ses ponts et plantes créent tout au long de l'année une atmosphère ouverte et communicative.

La galería cubierta de vidrio, una sala ajardinada y llena de luz no es solamente un amplio recinto de entrada para todas las 172 viviendas. Con sus arcadas, escaleras, puentes y plantas transmite una atmósfera abierta y comunicativa durante todo el año.

Wohn- und Geschäftshaus
Apartment and Office Block

Robert Meyer, Erich Gassmann

2003
Westendstraße 240
Laim

www.rmarchitekten.de

Das Grundstück am Pfaffenhofener Platz liegt zwischen der inhomogenen Bebauung im Norden und der Bebauung im Süden. Der neue zeilenförmige Baukörper fügt sich in die Umgebung ein, die Veränderung der städtebaulichen Situation wird mit einem Turm betont.

The site at Pfaffenhofener Platz is situated between the non-homogeneous building in the north and building in the south. The new structure is like a single line, merging with the surroundings; the alteration of the urban planning situation is emphasized by a tower.

Le terrain de la Pfaffenhofener Platz se situe entre le complexe de bâtiments non homogènes du nord et un ensemble de constructions au sud. Le nouveau corps de bâtiment en ligne s'intègre dans l'environnement, le changement de la situation urbanistique est souligné par une tour.

El terreno en la Pfaffenhofener Platz está situado entre la edificación no homogénea en el norte y la edificación en el sur. El cuerpo arquitectónico nuevo en forma de línea se inserta en el entorno, la modificación de la situación urbana es acentuada por la torre.

Wohnen im Turm

Living in a Tower

Binnberg + Eberle Design + Architektur
a.k.a. Ingenieure (SE)

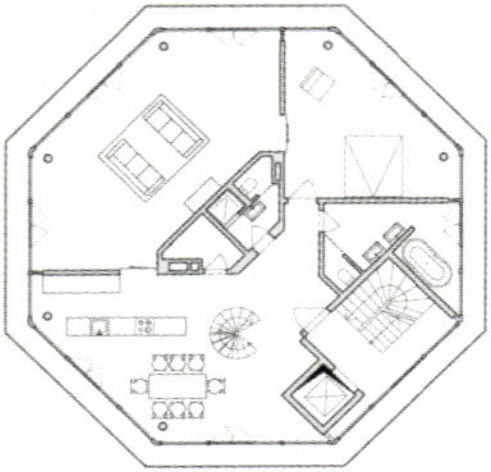

2005
Claude-Lorrain-Straße 26
Untergiesing-Harlaching

www.kunst-bunker.de
www.binnberg-eberle.de

Die Umgestaltung eines Hochbunkers aus dem Zweiten Weltkrieg in Wohn- und Arbeitsbereiche hat durchaus Vorbildcharakter. Für den achteckigen Betonklotz mit 2,20 Meter dicken Mauern ist neben deutlichen Fassadenveränderungen auch ein moderner Aufbau mit einem oder zwei Geschossen vorgesehen.

The remodeling of living and working zones in a World War Two bunker has certainly set an example. In addition to obvious changes in the façades, the plan for the octagonal concrete block, which has 2.2 meter thick walls, is also to include a modern extension with one or two floors.

La transformation d'un haut bunker de la deuxième guerre mondiale en zone d'habitat et de travail a certainement caractère d'exemple. Il est prévu de modifier radicalement la façade et de construire une extension moderne en surélévation de un ou deux étages sur ce bloc de béton octogonal aux murs de 2,20 mètres d'épaisseur.

La reforma de un búnker alto de la Segunda Guerra Mundial en recintos de viviendas y trabajo posee un carácter ejemplar en su totalidad. Para la mole de cemento octogonal con muros de 2,20 metros de grosor también está prevista, junto a claras modificaciones de la fachada, una ampliación moderna de una o dos plantas.

Wohnanlage Duelferstraße

Residential Site

Guggenbichler + Netzer Architekten
IB Hagl (SE)

2005
Duelferstraße 29-31
Hasenbergl

www.guggenbichler-netzer.de

Das hohe flache Gebäude in der Nähe des Feldmochinger Ackers beinhaltet unterschiedliche Wohnungstypen, die über Laubengänge zugänglich sind. Der Bau wird durch außen liegende Treppenhäuser und Aufzugstürme gegliedert und die Fassade durch Balkone und farbige Schiebeläden aufgelockert.

The tall, flat building near Feldmochinger Feld includes various styles of apartments, which are accessible by access balconies. The building is structured by external staircases and elevator shafts and the façade is more relaxed due to balconies and colorful manual shutters.

Le bâtiment haut et plat situé à proximité du Feldmochinger Acker se constitue de divers types d'appartements accessibles par des pergolas. La construction est structurée par des escaliers et des ascenseurs extérieurs, la façade est adoucie par des balcons et des volets coulissants de couleur.

El edificio alto y planto cercano al Feldmochinger Acker incluye diferentes tipos de viviendas que son accesibles por unas arcadas. La construcción se estructura por los huecos de las escaleras situadas afuera y por las torres de ascensores y la fachada está ahuecada por balcones y tiendas desplazables en color.

Wohngebäude Theresienhöhe

RPM Architekten

2003
August-Kühn-Straße 2
Schwanthaler Höhe

www.rpm-architekten.de

Die Gebäude bilden eine Mischform aus Blockrandbebauung und Einzelhäusern. Während an den Grundstücksgrenzen gerade verlaufende Fassaden die Straßenräume klar definieren, entwickeln sich durch die gegliederten Hofseiten der versetzten Baukörper unterschiedlich zugeschnittene öffentliche Freiräume.

The buildings are a hybrid combination of regular construction and individual blocks. While the straight line of the façades clearly defines the street areas at the periphery of the site, the structured courtyard zones of the displaced buildings develop different sizes of public, open spaces.

Les bâtiments forment un mélange de blocs et de maisons individuelles. Tandis que des façades rectilignes placées aux limites du terrain définissent clairement le domaine de la rue, les corps de bâtiments agencés en décalage du coté cour dessinent des espaces publics de tailles différentes.

Los edificios forman una mezcla de edificación de bloques al margen y de casas individuales. Las fachadas que recorren rectas las fronteras de los terrenos definen claramente los espacios de la calle mientras que los espacios públicos libres, cortados de diferente modo, se desarrollan por los lados del patio estructurados de los elementos arquitectónicos desplazados.

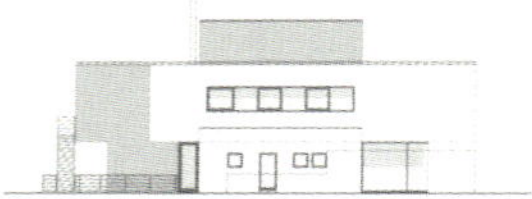

2 Villen

Jürke Architekten

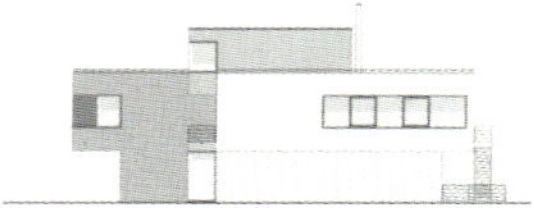

2002

Bogenhausen

www.jarch.de

Der Entwurf zweier Villen mit Pool wurde vom Baumbestand des Grundstücks bestimmt. Die Baukörper vermitteln den Eindruck, als würden sie sich ineinander schieben – trotz der dazwischen stehenden Kastanienbäume. Große Glasflächen binden die Natur in den Wohnraum ein.

The design for two villas with a swimming pool was controlled by the trees standing on this plot. The buildings give the impression of pushing into to each other—despite the chestnut trees standing between them. Large glass surfaces connect nature with living space.

Le projet des deux villas avec piscine est déterminé par l'implantation des arbres sur le terrain. Les bâtiments donnent l'impression de s'emboîter malgré la présence des châtaigniers s'intercalant entre eux. De grandes surfaces vitrées intègrent la nature dans l'espace d'habitation.

El plan de dos villas con piscina fue determinado por las existencias de árboles del terreno. Los cuerpos arquitectónicos transmiten la impresión de encajarse unos en otros a pesar de los castaños situados entre ellos. Las grandes superficies de vidrio integran la naturaleza en las viviendas.

Wohnturm Park Plaza

Residential Tower

Steidle + Partner
Seeberger, Friedl und Partner (SE), Hochtief Construction (SE)

2002
Hans-Dürrmeyer-Weg 2-4
Schwanthaler Höhe

www.steidle-partner.de

Der Wohnturm ist wichtiger Bestandteil des für die Theresienhöhe erarbeiteten Gesamtkonzepts. Die Fassade wird durch schubladenartig hervorragende Balkone und Dachterrassen geprägt, der Turm überragt die umliegenden Bauten deutlich und setzt mit seiner starken Farbigkeit einen markanten Akzent.

The residential tower is an important element of the overall design that was worked out for the Theresienhöhe. The façade is characterized by fantastic balconies, which look like drawers, and by roof terraces. The tower clearly soars above the surrounding buildings and its strong colours set an impressive tone.

La tour est un élément fondamental du concept général élaboré pour le projet Theresienhöhe. La façade est marquée par les balcons saillant comme des tiroirs et par les terrasses du toit, la tour domine les constructions des alentours et ses couleurs vives ajoutent une note originale.

La torre de viviendas es una parte esencial importante del plan general elaborado para los Theresienhöhen. La fachada está marcada por balcones salientes a modo de cajones y terrazas, la torre sobresale claramente de las edificaciones de los alrededores marcando la pauta característica con su fuerte coloración.

Münchener Rückversicherung

Baumschlager & Eberle Architekten
FSIT – Friedrich Straß (SE)

2001
Gedonstraße 10-12
Schwabing

www.muenchenerrueck.de
www.baumschlager-eberle.com

Ein massiver Betonbau aus den 60er Jahren wurde in einen modernen, grün schimmernden Firmensitz verwandelt. Aus einem geschlossenen Block wurde ein Ensemble mit Lichthöfen und Rücksprüngen, das sich gut in seine Umgebung einpasst. Für die Innengestaltung wurden namhafte Künstler hinzugezogen.

A 1960s solid concrete block was transformed into a modern, green shimmering company headquarters. An ensemble with light courtyards and recesses was made out of a closed block and fits well into its environment. Reputable artists were attracted to work on the interior design.

La construction en béton massive des années 60 a été transformée en siège de société moderne, vert et brillant. Le bloc fermé est devenu un ensemble pourvu de cours intérieures et de retraits s'intégrant bien à son environnement. Des artistes de renom ont conçu l'aménagement intérieur.

Una edificación masiva de hormigón de los años 60 fue transformada en la moderna sede de una empresa reluciendo en verde. Un bloque cerrado se convirtió en un conjunto con patios de luz y entrantes que encaja bien en su entorno. Para la configuración interior se consultó a artistas de renombre.

Bürozentrum Nymphenburger Straße 3

Office Center

Betz Architekten Planungsgesellschaft

2003
Nymphenburger Straße 3
Maxvorstadt

www.nymphe3.de
www.betz-architekten.de

Die sieben Einzelgebäude wurden als Ensemble auf einem ehemaligen Industriegrundstück errichtet, das spitzwinklige Torgebäude setzt in der Gruppe einen wichtigen Akzent. Den Mittelpunkt der Anlage bilden vier Baukörper, die sich um einen begehbaren, begrünten Innenhof mit Café-Pavillon und Wasserbecken gruppieren.

The seven individual buildings were built as an ensemble on a former industrial site, an acute-angled gate-house introduces an important note into the group. The center of the site is formed by four buildings, which are grouped around an accessible, leafy inner courtyard with a café pavillion and water basin.

Les sept édifices indépendants forment un ensemble sur l'ancien terrain industriel, le bâtiment d'accueil aux angles aigus se détache du groupe. Quatre constructions se groupant autour d'une cour intérieure verte et accessible, pourvue d'un pavillon-café et d'un bassin, sont le point central du projet.

Los siete edificios independientes fueron erigidos como un conjunto en un antiguo terreno industrial, el edificio del portal, de ángulos agudos, marca una pauta importante en el grupo. El centro de la instalación lo forman cuatro cuerpos arquitectónicos que se agrupan en torno a un patio interior transitable ajardinado con un pabellón con un café y un estanque.

Hypo Vereinsbank

Extension

Betz Architekten Planungsgesellschaft
OPB Obermeyer, Planen + Beraten (SE)

1999
Arabellastraße 13
Bogenhausen

www.hypovereinsbank.de
www.betz-architekten.de

Die Erweiterung des Hochhauses aus den 70ern beinhaltet eine Veranstaltungshalle, zu der sich die Büros öffnen. Der eigentlichen Glasfassade ist eine zweite aus flexiblen Glaspaneelen vorgelagert, die den Lichteinfall regulieren. Die Lichtinstallation von Dan Flavin hüllt die Haupttreppe in unwirkliches Licht von wechselnder Farbe.

The extension to a 1970s sky scraper includes a conference center, which opens out into office space. The actual glass façade is set back from a second flexible layer of glass panels, which regulate the light flow. The light installation by Dan Flavin covers the main staircase in an unreal light that changes colour.

L'aménagement de l'immeuble des années 70 comprend une salle de conférence communiquant avec les bureaux. A la façade en verre existante est rajoutée un deuxième panneau en verre flexible qui régularise l'entrée de la lumière. L'installation lumineuse de Dan Flavin enveloppe l'escalier principal d'une lumière irréelle à la couleur changeante.

La ampliación del rascacielos de los años 70 contiene una sala de actos hacia la que se abren las oficinas. Superpuesta a la verdadera fachada de vidrio hay colocada una segunda de paneles flexibles de vidrio que regulan la entrada de luz. La instalación de luz de Dan Flavin cubre la escalera principal con una luz irreal de color cambiante.

Swiss Re Hauptverwaltung

Admininstrative Headquarters

BRT Architekten Bothe Richter Teherani

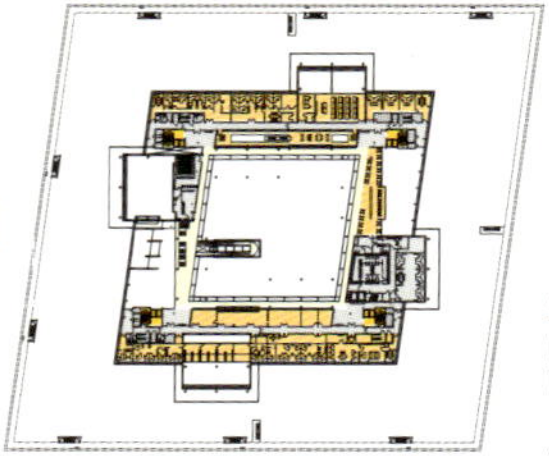

2001
Dieselstraße 11
Unterföhring

www.swissre.com
www.brt.de

Lichte Büroräume, gleichzeitig bauliche Geschlossenheit und Sichtschutz – dieser vermeintliche Widerspruch hebt sich durch Hightech-Glasfassaden auf. Das spektakuläre Verwaltungsgebäude der „Swiss Re" schwebt dabei scheinbar in der Luft: Die aufgeständerten Bürotrakte wirken wie vom Boden abgehoben.

Light office space teams up with an enclosed structure and sheltered outlook—this apparent contradiction is suspended because of the high-tech glass façades. The spectacular administrative headquarters of "Swiss Re" seems to float in mid-air: the additional levels of the office wings appear to be lifted off the ground.

Bureaux lumineux, unité architectonique et protection visuelle – cette prétendue contradiction est abolie par les façades en verre de technologie innovatrice. Le spectaculaire bâtiment administratif « Swiss re » semble planer dans les airs : les blocs de bureaux sur piliers paraissent s'élever du sol.

Las luminosas salas de oficinas, al mismo tiempo una unidad arquitectónica y una protección visual; esta supuesta contradicción se suprime por medio de las fachadas de vidrio de alta tecnología. El espectacular edificio de la administración de "Swiss Re" flota aparentemente en el aire: Las alas de oficinas sobre soportes parece como si estuviesen levantadas del suelo.

Uptown Munich

Ingenhoven Overdiek und Partner, ATP Architekten und Ingenieure
Burggraf, Weichinger & Partner (SE)

2004
Georg-Brauchle-Ring 50-52
Schwabing

www.uptownmuenchen.com
www.ingenhoven-overdiek.de

Die Gebäudekomposition besteht aus einem 146 Meter hohen Hochhaus und vier siebengeschossigen Campusgebäuden, deren gebäudeverbindende Lamellendachkonstruktion mit dem Boulevard die Ost-West-Achse beschreibt. Das Hochhaus fügt sich als neues Wahrzeichen in die Silhouette der Stadt München ein.

The building composition is formed by one 146 meter high sky scraper and four seven-storey campus buildings, whose blade roof construction is a connecting link for the buildings, which form the site's east-west axis, along with the avenue. The sky scraper merges with Munich's city skyline as a new landmark.

La composition architecturale inclut un immeuble de 146 mètres de hauteur et quatre bâtiments universitaires de sept étages dont la construction en lamelle du toit les relie entre eux formant avec le boulevard l'axe est-ouest. L'immeuble s'intègre dans la silhouette de la ville de Munich en tant que nouvel emblème.

La composición de edificios consiste en un rascacielos de 146 metros de altura y cuatro edificios de campus de siete plantas cuya construcción de tejado de láminas que une los edificios describe el eje este-oeste con el boulevard. El rascacielos se integra en la silueta de la ciudad de Munich como un nuevo símbolo característico.

ClassiCon

Jürke Architekten

2002
Sigmund-Riefler-Bogen 3
Messestadt Riem

www.classicon.com
www.jarch.de

Das Gebäude hebt sich bewusst gegen die Nachbarbebauung ab. Mit seinen harten Kanten, scharfen Linien und glatten Sichtbetonflächen hält es Distanz zu den ausgestellten Möbeln. Der blockhafte Baukörper öffnet sich großzügig nach Süden hin, Showroom und Büros befinden sich dahinter.

The building is deliberately distinguished from the neighbouring structures. The hard edges, sharp lines and smooth, exposed concrete surfaces maintain a distance to the furniture on display. The block-style structure is more spacious towards the south and the showroom and offices are located behind.

Le bâtiment se détache consciemment des constructions voisines. Ses bords durs, ses lignes acérées et ses surfaces de béton apparent le maintiennent à distance des meubles exposés. Le bloc architectonique s'ouvre généreusement vers le sud, la salle d'exposition et les bureaux se situent derrière.

El edificio se destaca conscientemente sobre la edificación vecina. Con sus cantos duros, las líneas agudas y las superficies llanas de hormigón liso mantiene la distancia con los muebles expuestos. El cuerpo arquitectónico a modo de bloque se abre generosamente hacia el sur, la sala de exposiciones y las oficinas se encuentran detrás.

Avalon Bürogebäude MK4

Office Block

Ortner & Ortner
Assmann Beraten + Planen (SE)

2003
Radlkoferstraße 16
Schwanthaler Höhe

www.ortner-ortner.de

Auffällig an dem fünfstöckigen Gebäude ist seine prägnante Fassade. Aus der cremefarbenen Natursteinfassade springen reliefartige Krustenplatten aus Juramarmor hervor. So legt sich über die rationale Bürofassade eine Art steinernes Fell. Nicht ganz glatt, verleiht es dem Gebäude die in dieser Lage nötige Präsenz.

The distinctive façade is the striking factor about the five-storey building. Plates in relief-style and made of marble from the Jura mountains project out of the cream-colored natural stone. In this way, a sort of stone animal skin covers the rational office block façade. Since it is not entirely smooth, the surface puts the building on the map in this location.

Cet édifice de cinq étages attire l'attention par sa façade caractéristique. De la façade en pierre naturelle de couleur crème se détachent des plaques en relief, en marbre brut du Jura. Une sorte de fourrure en pierre habille ainsi la façade rationnelle des bureaux. Par son aspect non lisse, elle donne au bâtiment la présence qui lui est nécessaire.

En el edificio de cinco plantas llama la atención su fachada característica. De la fachada de piedra natural en color crema resaltan las placas con costra de mármol jurásico a modo de relieve. Así se coloca una especie de piel de piedra sobre la racional fachada de oficinas. No siendo muy lisa dota al edificio de la presencia necesaria en esta zona.

Deutsche Bahn AG Betriebszentrale

Operations Headquarters

SIAT Architecting
SSP Sailer Stepan und Partner (SE)

2000
Richelstraße 3
Neuhausen

www.db.de
www.siat.de

Das Netzgebäude ist virtuelles Zentrum des Bahnverkehrs in der Region Süd. Aufgrund von Sicherheitsanforderungen ist das Gebäude von außen hermetisch abgeschlossen. Eine monochrome Lamellenstruktur umgibt das Gebäude und lässt den Eindruck eines technisch-abstrakten Objektes ohne Bezug zu seiner Umgebung entstehen.

The network building is a virtual headquarters for train traffic in the southern region. Due to security requirements, the building is hermetically sealed from the outside. A monochrome blade structure surrounds the building and creates the impression of a technical and abstract object without any relation to its environment.

Ce bâtiment est le centre virtuel du trafic ferroviaire de la région sud. En raison des exigences de sécurité, le bâtiment est hermétiquement fermé à l'extérieur. Une structure en lamelles monochrome entoure l'édifice et fait penser à un objet technique et abstrait sans relation avec son environnement.

El edificio de red es el centro virtual del tráfico férreo en la región del sur. Debido a las exigencias de seguridad el edificio está cerrado herméticamente por fuera. Una estructura de láminas monocromática rodea el edificio y hace producir la impresión de un objeto técnico abstracto sin referencia con su entorno.

Deutsche Bundesbank

Behnisch + Partner
Schmidhuber + Partner

1998
Leopoldstraße 234
Milbertshofen

www.bundesbank.de
www.behnisch.com
www.schmidhuber.de

Ein transparent wirkendes Bankgebäude zu schaffen war Ausgangspunkt des Entwurfs. Die Innenarchitektur steigert die Formensprache zu einer spielerischen und lichten Rauminszenierung, in der sich öffentliche und halböffentliche Bereiche überlagern.

The initiative for the design was to create a transparent-looking bank building. The interior architecture intensifies the form language to a playful and light staging of space, in which public and semi-public areas overlap one another.

Le point de départ du projet était de concevoir un édifice bancaire donnant une impression de transparence. L'architecture intérieure intensifie le langage des formes et met en scène un espace de jeu et de lumière dans lequel les zones publiques et semi-publiques se superposent.

Crear un edificio de bancos que pareciese transparente fue el punto de partida del proyecto. La arquitectura interior eleva el lenguaje de formas a una escenificación del espacio juguetona y luminosa en la que se superponen los ámbitos público y semipúblico.

msg systems AG Hauptverwaltung

Administrative Headquarters

Hein Goldstein Architekt

2003
Robert-Bürkle-Straße 1
Ismaning

www.msg.de
www.goldstein-architekten.de

Große Glasflächen, Stahl und Naturstein prägen das Software-Entwicklungs- und Verwaltungsgebäude. Interessante Raumperspektiven, helle und großzügige Zimmer schaffen angenehme Arbeitsbedingungen. Unterschiedlich gestaltete Innenhöfe bieten den Mitarbeitern Aufenthaltsraum und Kommunikationsfläche.

Large glass areas, steel and natural stone influence this software development and administrative building. Interesting spatial perspectives, light and spacious rooms create pleasant working conditions. Various different designs for inner courtyards provide the employees with a recreation room and communication zone.

De grandes surfaces vitrées, de l'acier et de la pierre naturelle empreignent l'édifice du développement logiciel et de l'administration. Des perspectives d'espace intéressantes, des pièces lumineuses et généreuses créent des conditions agréables de travail. Des cours intérieures variées offrent des espaces de repos et de communication aux employés.

Las grandes superficies de vidrio, el acero y la piedra natural caracterizan el edificio de administración, software y desarrollo. Las perspectivas del espacio interesantes, las habitaciones iluminadas y amplias crean unas condiciones de trabajo agradables. Los patios interiores configurados de modos distintos ofrecen a los empleados una sala de descanso y superficie de comunicación.

HighLight Business Towers

Murphy / Jahn

2004
Mies-van-der-Rohe-Straße 4-10
Schwabing

www.highlight-towers.com
www.murphyjahn.com

Zwei schlanke 113 und 126 Meter hohe Türme, verbunden durch drei Brücken aus Glas und Stahl, positionieren sich unübersehbar am Münchner Tor. Die unter technologischen und ökologischen Aspekten gestaltete Fassade gibt dem Gebäude eine kristallin-glatte Erscheinung. Es wirkt leicht und transparent.

Two slim, 113- and 126-meter tall towers, connected by three bridges of glass and steel unmistakeably take position at Münchner Tor. The façade was designed with technological and ecological aspects in mind and gives the building a smooth, crystalline appearance. The structure looks light and transparent.

Deux tours effilées de 113 et 126 mètres de haut reliées par trois ponts en acier et verre se positionnent devant la Münchner Tor. La façade conçue en respectant les aspects technologiques et écologiques donne au bâtiment une apparence lisse et cristalline. Il semble léger et transparent.

Dos torres delgadas de 113 y 126 metros de altura, unidas por medio de tres puentes de vidrio y acero, se posicionan inconfundiblemente frente a la Münchner Tor. La fachada diseñada bajo aspectos tecnológicos y ecológicos otorga al edificio una apariencia cristalina lisa. Produce un efecto ligero y transparente.

Amt für Abfallwirtschaft

Office for Waste Disposal

Ackermann + Partner Architekten
Schlaich, Bergermann und Partner
a.k.a. Ingenieure (SE)

2000
Georg-Brauchle-Ring 29
Schwabing

www.awm.muenchen.de
www.sbp.de
www.ackermann-partner.com

Das Amt für Abfallwirtschaft besteht aus drei Bauteilen: einem zehngeschossigen Verwaltungsgebäude, einer Werkstatt und einem Carport. Der Carport wird von einer filigranen Membrankonstruktion überspannt, die mit ihrem teflonbeschichteten, lichtdurchlässigen Glasfasergewebe wie ein luftiges Zelt wirkt.

The Office for Waste Disposal consists of three building elements: a ten-storey administrative building, a workshop and car port. The car port is overarched by a filigree membrane construction, which looks like an airy tent and is made of teflon layers and glassfiber cloth, which let the light through.

L'office pour la gestion des déchets se compose de trois éléments de construction : un bâtiment administratif de dix étages, un atelier et un carport. Le carport est recouvert d'une construction-membrane filigrane en fibre de verre enrobée de téflon laissant passer l'air, qui ressemble à une tente aérienne.

La Oficina de Reciclaje consta de tres elementos arquitectónicos: un edificio de administración de diez plantas, un taller y un carport. El carport es cubierto con una construcción de membrana en filigrana que con su tejido transparente de fibra de vidrio revestida de teflón parece una carpa ligera.

Allguth Tankstelle Gläserne Waschstraße

Gas Station

Haack + Höpfner Architekten
a.k.a. Ingenieure (SE)

2004
Landsberger Straße 2
Germering

www.allguth.de
www.haackhoepfner.de

Eine puristisch gehaltene gläserne Fassade umhüllt schnörkellos und funktional eine 50 Meter lange Autowaschanlage. Die gläserne Außenwand schirmt so die Tankstelle nach außen ab und wird zu einem sich im Tages- und Kunstlicht scheinbar permanent ändernden Objekt.

A purist glass façade that has no frills and is functional surrounds a 50 meter long car-wash plant. This is how the glass exterior wall shelters the gas station from outside and turns into an object that appears permanently to change in daylight as well as artificial light.

Une façade en verre de style puriste enveloppe fonctionnellement et sans fioriture une station de lavage pour voitures qui s'étend sur une longueur de 50 mètres. Le mur en verre extérieur protège la station-service du dehors et devient un objet changeant en permanence sous l'effet de la lumière du jour et de l'éclairage artificiel.

Una fachada purista de vidrio envuelve, sin decoración y de un modo funcional, un tren de lavado de coches de 50 metros de longitud. La pared exterior de vidrio protege así la gasolinera hacia el exterior convirtiéndose en un objeto que en apariencia cambia permanentemente bajo luz natural y artificial.

Einfahrt Waschstra

Projekthaus der BMW AG

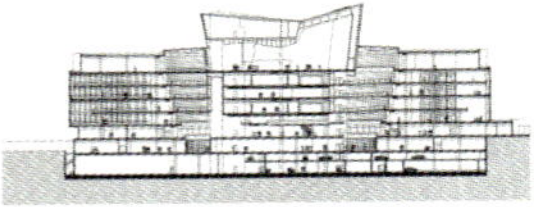

Project House

Henn Architekten
SSP Sailer Stepan und Partner (SE)

2004
Knorrstraße 147
Milbertshofen

www.bmw.com
www.henn.com

Vier Gebäudemodule, zu Doppelgeschossen zusammengefasst, gruppieren sich um ein kreisförmiges Atrium. Die Gebäude sind durch Brücken miteinander verbunden und werden von einem Glasdach überspannt. Den oberen Abschluss des 45 Meter hohen Hauptgebäudes bildet ein multifunktionaler Präsentationsraum.

Four building modules, joined together to make double storeys, are grouped around a circular atrium. The buildings are connected with each other by bridges and are overarched by a glass roof. The upper end of the 45 meter high main building forms a multi-purpose presentation room.

Quatre modules architecturaux de deux étages chacun se regroupent autour d'un patio circulaire. Les bâtiments sont reliés par des ponts et recouverts par un toit en verre. La partie supérieure de l'édifice principal de 45 mètres de haut abrite une salle de présentation multifonctions.

Cuatro módulos de edificios, reunidos en plantas dobles, se agrupan en torno a un patio circular. Los edificios están unidos entre ellos por puentes y fueron cubiertos por un tejado de vidrio. El extremo superior del edificio principal, de 45 metros de altura, lo constituye una sala de presentaciones de múltiples funciones.

Pinakothek der Moderne

Stephan Braunfels Architekten

2002
Kunstareal Barer Straße 40
Maxvorstadt

www.pinakothek-der-moderne.de
www.braunfels-architekten.de

Der Museumsneubau ist von der Innenstadt als auch von Alter und Neuer Pinakothek aus zugänglich. Von den Eingängen aus gelangt der Besucher in eine zentrale Glaskuppel-gedeckte Halle, von der aus die drei Ebenen mit Treppen erschlossen werden. Dadurch zieht sich eine diagonale Achse durch das ganze Gebäude.

The new museum building can be accessed from the city center, as well as from the Old and New Pinakothek. From the entrances, the visitor arrives in a main hall covered by a glass dome. From here, three storeys are accessed by stairs and this means a diagonal axis runs through the entire building.

Le nouveau musée est accessible du centre-ville ainsi que de l'ancienne et de la nouvelle pinacothèque. Les entrées mènent le visiteur à une salle recouverte d'une coupole en verre dont les trois niveaux sont reliés par des escaliers. Par là, un axe diagonal traverse tout le bâtiment.

A la nueva edificación del museo se accede tanto desde el centro como desde la Antigua y la Nueva Pinacoteca. Desde las entradas el visitante llega a una sala central cubierta por una cúpula de cristal desde la cual se cerraron los tres niveles con escaleras. De esta manera un eje diagonal discurre por todo el edificio.

Danner Rotunde in der Pinakothek der Moderne

Landau + Kindelbacher Architekten – Innenarchitekten

2004
Kunstareal Barer Straße 40
Maxvorstadt

www.pinakothek.de
www.landaukindelbacher.de

In den Ausstellungsräumen tritt die Architektur in den Hintergrund. Der spannungsvolle Raum ist geometrisch beschrieben ein 180° umfassendes Kreisringsegment. Die archaische Anmutung der Raumhülle mit den Betonstützen und der Sichtbetondecke steht im Kontrast zu den filigranen Ausstellungsstücken.

The architecture fades into the background in the exhibition rooms. To describe the tension-filled room geometrically, it forms a 180° encompassing annulus segment. The shell of the rooms has an archaic tone with concrete pillars and an exposed concrete ceiling, which is in contrast to the filigree exhibition pieces.

Dans les salles d'exposition, l'architecture passe au second plan. La pièce très contrastée forme géométriquement un segment de cercle de 180°. Le charme archaïque de l'enveloppe posée sur des piliers en béton et le plafond en béton apparent contrastent avec les pièces légères de l'exposition.

La arquitectura pasan a un segundo plano en las salas de exposiciones. Descrito geométricamente, el inquietante espacio es un segmento circular que abarca 180°. La elegancia arcaica del revestimiento del espacio con los soportes de hormigón y la cobertura de hormigón liso está en contraste con los objetos expuestos en filigrana.

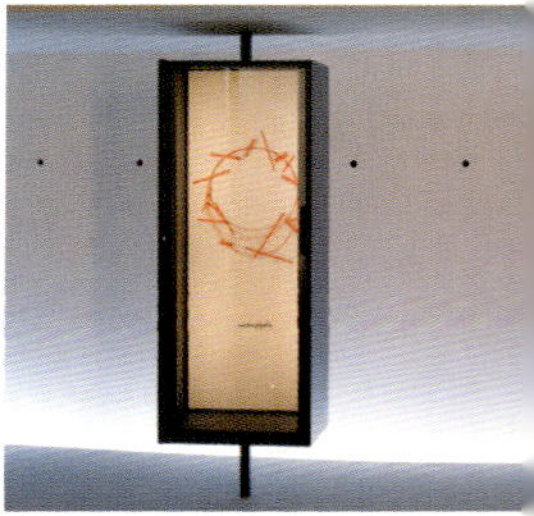

laus Arck Vol
aezner Alexar
riedrich Bec
oris Betz Dav
oekhoudt Rud
orun Bülow-H
utler Alexan
ecchetto Ant
argaret De Pa
obert Ebendor
nna Fraling W
röhlich Anton
e Andi Gut Re
iramatsu Elis
ino Hiroshi I
ohn Hermann J
ered Kaminski
ruger Winfrie
ritz Maierhof
runo Martinaz
iko Minewaki
anfred Nissl
avan Sigurd P
aren Pontopp
olfgang Rahs
ann Fabrice Sc
inger Hubert

Herz Jesu Kirche

Church

Allmann Sattler Wappner Architekten

2000
Lachnerstraße 8
Neuhausen

www.herzjesu-muenchen.de
www.allmannsattlerwappner.de

Der Glaskubus ist nicht unmittelbar als Kirche zu erkennen. Die Kirche wurde als Raum im Raum konzipiert. Eine Glashülle mit gigantischem Tor beherbergt einen hölzernen Schrein – den eigentlichen Kirchenraum. Gefiltertes Licht erzeugt im Innenraum eine sakrale Atmosphäre.

The glass cube is not immediately recognizable as a church. The church was designed as a room within a room. A glass cave with a gigantic gate houses a wooden shrine, which is the real church. Filtered light produces a sacred atmosphere in the interior.

Dans le cube en verre, on ne reconnaît pas immédiatement une église. L'église a été conçue comme un espace à l'intérieur d'un autre espace. Une enveloppe en verre pourvue d'une porte gigantesque abrite une pièce en bois qui est la véritable église. Une lumière filtrée crée une atmosphère sacrée dans l'espace intérieur.

El cubo de vidrio no puede reconocerse directamente como una iglesia. La iglesia fue planeada como un espacio dentro del espacio. Un revestimiento de vidrio con un portal gigantesco alberga un cofre de madera, el verdadero espacio de la iglesia. La luz filtrada produce una atmósfera sacra en el interior.

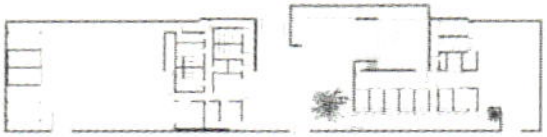

Aussegnungshalle

Funeral Parlor

Meck Architekten
Dieter Herrschmann (SE)

2000
Straße am Mitterfeld 68
Messestadt Riem

www.meck-architekten.de

Die Friedhofsanlage besteht aus Beton, Naturstein, Eiche und Stahl. Ein Steindach deckt die Aussegnungshalle, einen glatten Eichenholzkubus. Ein direkter Ausblick wurde vermieden. So erhält der Bau einen introvertierten, sakralen Charakter. Zudem schafft eine goldglänzende Wasserfläche eine meditative Atmosphäre.

The site of the cemetery is built out of concrete, natural stone, oak and steel. A stone roof covers the funeral parlor, which is a smooth, solid oak cube structure. Any direct views to the outside have been avoided, so the building keeps an introspective, sacred character. Additionally, a meditative mood is created by a gold-gleaming water area.

L'édifice du cimetière se compose de béton, de pierre naturelle, de chêne et d'acier. Un toit en pierre recouvre la salle mortuaire constituée d'un cube lisse en bois de chêne. Une perspective directe a été évitée. De cette manière, la construction s'empreint d'un caractère introverti et sacré. En outre, une surface aquatique dorée ajoute une atmosphère méditative.

El recinto del cementerio consta de hormigón, piedra natural, roble y acero. Un tejado de piedra cubre el tanatorio, un cubo liso de madera de roble. Se evitó una vista directa. Así, la edificación recibe un carácter introvertido, sacro. Además, una superficie de agua con un brillo dorado crea una atmósfera de meditación.

Allerheiligen Hofkirche

Church

Guggenbichler + Netzer Architekten
Ingenieurbüro HKM (SE)

2003
Residenzstraße 1
Altstadt

www.guggenbichler-netzer.de

Die Kirche wurde in einen vielfältig nutzbaren, zeitgemäßen Veranstaltungsraum für etwa 400 Besucher umgebaut. Alle Eingriffe sind mit größter Zurückhaltung, aber dennoch in klarer Formensprache erfolgt; dem entspricht auch die Beschränkung auf wenige Materialien, meist Stahl, Glas, Beton.

The church was remodeled into a multi-functional contemporary conference hall for about 400 visitors. Great restraint has been exercised with any interventions, which still keep a clear form language. The restriction to a few materials, mostly steel, glass, concrete also corresponds to this approach.

L'église a été transformée en salle contemporaine utilisable de diverses manières et pouvant abriter 400 visiteurs. Toutes les modifications ont été faites avec extrême modération mais dans un langage des formes clair auquel correspond une utilisation limitée des matériaux, le plus souvent de l'acier, du verre et du béton.

La iglesia fue reformada en una sala de actos para aproximadamente 400 visitantes de utilización variada y conforme a la época. Todas las intervenciones se efectuaron con la mayor cautela pero, no obstante, con un claro lenguaje de formas; a esto corresponde también la limitación a unos pocos materiales, mayormente acero, vidrio y hormigón.

TU München
Fakultät für Maschinenwesen Garching
Technical University

Henn Architekten
SSP Sailer Stepan und Partner (SE)

2003
Boltzmannstraße 15
Garching

www.mw.tu-muenchen.de
www.henn.com

Der neue Hochschulkomplex wurde in Bereiche aufgegliedert, die entweder der Kommunikation oder der Konzentration dienen sollen. An die Fakultätsstraße sind Bibliothek, Hörsäle, Seminargebäude, Läden und Cafeteria angebunden. Zwischen den einzelnen Institutsbauten befinden sich Zeichen- und Seminarräume.

The new site of the university building was structured into areas that are either meant to serve communication or concentration. The library, lecture theaters, seminar buildings, shops and cafeteria have been linked with the Fakultätsstraße. Drawing and seminar rooms are located between the individual institute buildings.

Le nouveau complexe universitaire a été divisé en plusieurs domaines servant, soit à la communication, soit à la concentration. La bibliothèque, les salles de cours, les bâtiments de travaux pratiques, les boutiques et la cafétéria communiquent avec la Fakultätsstraße. Des salles de travaux pratiques et de dessin sont disponibles entre les bâtiments de l'institut.

El nuevo complejo universitario fue organizado en recintos que han de servir o bien para la comunicación o para la concentración. A la Fakultätsstraße se encuentran enlazadas la biblioteca, las aulas, los edificios para las clases, las tiendas y la cafetería. Entre los edificios de los institutos se hallan las salas de dibujo y para cursos.

Fraunhofer Haus

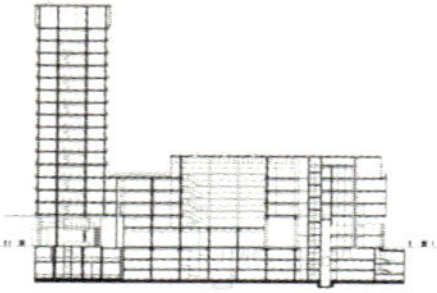

Henn Architekten
SSP Sailer Stepan und Partner (SE)

2003
Hansastraße 27c
Sendling

www.fraunhofer.de
www.henn.com

Das 65 Meter hohe Gebäude gehört zu den neuen, die Skyline prägenden Hochhäusern. Die grünliche Außenfassade des Turms und der Nebengebäude mit 380 computergesteuerten Glasklappen dient der Schallreduktion in der stark lärmbelasteten Umgebung und gleichzeitig der Belüftung der Büros.

The 65 meter tall building belongs to the new skyscrapers that rule the skyline. The greenish exterior façade of the tower and adjacent building with 380 computer-driven glass flaps is for noise reduction in an area that is heavily polluted by noise. The structure helps to ventilate the offices at the same time.

Cet édifice de 65 mètres de haut s'intègre dans la ligne d'horizon des hauts immeubles. La façade extérieure verdâtre de la tour et des bâtiments annexes pourvue de 380 panneaux en verre commandés par ordinateur est conçue pour isoler de l'environnement très bruyant, et pour la ventilation des bureaux.

El edificio de 65 metros de altura pertenece a los nuevos rascacielos que caracterizan la skyline. La fachada exterior verdosa de la torre y del edificio colindante con 380 tapas de vidrio dirigidas por ordenador sirve para reducir las ondas en el entorno de mucha contaminación sonora y, al mismo tiempo, como ventilación de las oficinas.

Akademie der Bildenden Künste

Academy of Visual Arts

Coop Himmelb(l)au

2005
Akademiestraße 2
Schwabing

www.adbk.de
www.coop-himmelblau.at

Das Konzept von Coop Himmelb(l)au sieht die Vernetzung der einzelnen funktionalen Bereiche in den verschiedenen Gebäudeteilen und damit auch der unterschiedlichen Fachbereiche selbst vor. Dies entspricht in idealer Weise den vielfältigen Bedürfnissen und Anforderungen kreativer Tätigkeiten.

The concept of Coop Himmelb(l)au is a plan for networking individual functional areas in the various building sections and therefore of the different specialized areas as well. In an ideal sense, this corresponds to the manifold needs and demands of creative initiatives.

Le concept de Coop Himmelb(l)au prévoit la liaison des domaines fonctionnels dans les différents éléments du bâtiment et donc des différentes sections. Il correspond de manière idéale aux besoins et aux diverses exigences relatives aux activités créatrices.

El plan de Coop Himmelb(l)au prevé la conexión de todos los ámbitos individuales funcionales en las diferentes partes del edificio y con ello también la de las distintas especialidades mismas. Esto corresponde de manera ideal a las necesidades variadas y los requerimientos de las actividades creativas.

Münchner Kammerspiele Probebühne

Munich Small Theater Rehearsal Stage

Peichl & Partner Architekten

2001
Falckenbergstraße 1
Altstadt

www.muenchner-kammerspiele.de
www.peichl-partner.at

Der helle, fast weiße Kubus beinhaltet drei Probebühnen. Im Gebäudeinneren fanden mehrere Räume mit verschiedenen Nutzungsmöglichkeiten Platz, die Hälfte davon unterhalb der Erdoberfläche. Unter der für Peichl typischen Glaspyramide befindet sich ein rundum verglaster Besprechungsraum.

The light, almost white cube houses three rehearsal stages. In the building's interior, there was space for several rooms with various possible uses, half of the rooms being underground. Below the glass pyramid, which is typical of Peichl style, there is a conference room made entirely out of glass.

Le cube clair et presque blanc abrite trois scènes de répétition. A l'intérieur du bâtiment, plusieurs salles offrent des possibilités variées d'utilisation, la moitié d'entre-elles se trouvent sous le niveau du sol. En dessous de la pyramide en verre typique à Peichl se trouve une salle de conférence toute en verre.

El cubo claro, casi blanco, contiene tres escenarios para ensayos. En el interior del edificio encontraron espacio varias salas con diferentes posibilidades de utilización, la mitad de ellas debajo de la superficie de la tierra. Debajo de la pirámide de vidrio típica de Peichl se halla una sala de conferencias completamente acristalada.

CUBE
Lichtkubus beim Designparcours
Light Cube at the Design Course

Meierei Innenarchitekten

2004
Prinzregentenstraße 3
Altstadt

www.designparcours.net
www.meierei.org

Das Konzept der begehbaren Installation ist, Design in seinen verschiedenen Qualitäten gegenüber zustellen. Realisiert wurde ein weißer, „schwebender" Lichtkubus. Für die Fassade kam das Material Styropor zum Einsatz. Die Blütenmotive wurden als Halbrelief aufgebracht und partiell hinterleuchtet.

The idea of the accessible installation is to confront design with its different qualities. A white, "swaying" light cube was achieved. Polystyrene was used for the façade. The floral bud motifs were introduced as semi-relief and partially illuminated with back-lighting.

Le concept de cette installation à accès libre est de présenter le design sous ses différents aspects qualitatifs. Un cube de lumière « flottant » a été réalisé. Pour la façade, le matériau polystyrène expansé a été privilégié. Le motif floral a été appliqué en semi-relief, souligné par un éclairage partiel à l'arrière-plan.

El plan para la instalación transitable es confrontar el diseño en sus diferentes cualidades. Se realizó un cubo de luz blanco "flotante". Para la fachada se utilizó el material del poliestireno. Los motivos florales se pusieron como semirelieves y se iluminaron parcialmente por detrás.

ZKMax

Hai Merlin-Studio für Architekten
a.k.a. Ingenieure (SE)

2004
Passage Altstadtring /
Maximilianstraße
Altstadt

www.zkmax.de
www.urbnet.de

Die Ende der 60er Jahre entstandene Unterführung wurde in einen öffentlichen Ort für Kunst verwandelt. Entstanden ist ein variables Raumgefüge, das mittels beweglicher Glaswände verschiedene Raumlösungen anbietet. Gelbe Lichtinstallationen markieren die ehemaligen Ein- und Ausgänge.

The subway, dating from the end of the 1960s, was transformed into a public place for art. A room structure was created to provide different space solutions by moving about the glass walls. Yellow light installations mark the old entrances and exits.

Le passage souterrain construit à la fin des années 60 a été transformé en un endroit public dédié à l'art. Les parois de verre mobiles permettent de varier la disposition de l'espace. Des éclairages de lumière jaune soulignent les anciennes entrées et sorties.

El paso subterráneo surgido a finales de los años 60 fue transformado en un lugar público para el arte. Surgió una estructura variable del espacio que ofrece diferentes soluciones para el espacio por medio de paredes de vidrio móviles. Las instalaciones de luces amarillas marcan las antiguas entradas y salidas.

ZKMax
www.ZKMax.de www.ZKMax.de

U-Bahnhof St. Quirin-Platz

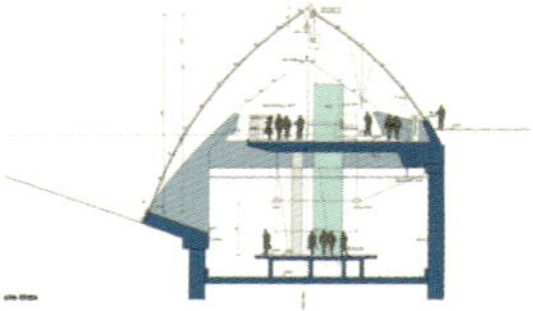

Subway Station

Hermann + Öttl Architekten
Ingenieurbüro Ulrich Elsner (SE)

1997
St. Quirin-Platz
Obergiesing

www.hermann-oettl.de

Die Halle wird durch eine muschelförmige Glaskuppel geprägt. Die extravagante Raumwirkung entsteht durch das durch die Kuppel einfallende Tageslicht und den Kontrast zwischen „Naturbelassenem“ und „Veredeltem“. Dieser skulpturalen Struktur stehen glatte, glänzende Materialien wie polierter Edelstahl, Glas und Naturstein gegenüber.

The hall is characterized by a shell-shaped glass dome. The extravagant effect of space is created by daylight pouring through the dome and the contrast of “nature's force” and “refinement”. As a contrast for this sculptural structure, there are smooth, shining materials like polished stainless steel, glass and natural stone.

Le hall se caractérise par sa coupole en verre en forme de coquillage. L'effet extravagant de l'espace est rendu par la lumière passant à travers la coupole et par le contraste entre le « naturel » et « l'élaboré ». Des matériaux brillants et lisses comme l'acier inoxydable poli, le verre et la pierre naturelle s'opposent à cette structure sculpturale.

La nave se caracteriza por una cúpula de cristal en forma de concha. El efecto extravagante del espacio surge debido a la luz natural que entra por la cúpula y por el contraste entre lo “natural” y lo “elaborado”. Frente a esta estructura escultural están los materiales lisos y brillantes como el acero noble pulido, el vidrio y la piedra natural.

Fußgängerbrücke

Pedestrian Bridge

Ackermann + Partner Architekten
Ingenieurbüro Christoph Ackermann (SE)

2003
Walter-Gropius-Straße
Schwabing

www.ackermann-partner.com

Die barrierefreie Fußgängerbrücke über die A9 wirkt wie ein Stadttor für den Autoverkehr. Ein filigraner Steg ist zwischen zwei Pfeiler gehängt, die Treppen und behindertengerechten Rampen nutzen den schmalen Randstreifen. Schmale LED Lichtröhren unterstützen die luftig-leichte Erscheinung der Brücke.

The pedestrian bridge is an open-access route across the A9 and acts like a city gate for road traffic. A filigree bridge is suspended between two pillars, whereas stairs and ramps for the disabled use the narrow strips at the edge. The bridge's airy and light appearance is promoted by narrow LED light strips.

Le pont pour piéton, sans barrière, passant au-dessus de l'autoroute A9 donne l'impression d'être la porte de la ville pour le trafic routier. Une passerelle légère est suspendue entre les deux piliers, les escaliers et les rampes pour handicapés utilisent les bordures étroites. Des tubes fins à diodes lumineuses accentuent l'apparence légère et aérienne du pont.

El puente peatonal sobre la autopista A9, libre de barreras arquitectónicas, parece la puerta de una ciudad para el tráfico rodado. Una pasarela en filigrana está colgada entre dos soportes, las escaleras y las rampas acondicionadas para minusválidos aprovechan las delgadas franjas del margen. Delgados tubos luminosos efecto LED apoyan la apariencia aérea y ligera del puente.

Neue Messe München
Extension

New Trade Fair Munich

Kaup Jesse Hofmayr Werner, Architekten

2004
Am Messesee 2
Messestadt Riem

www.messe-muenchen.de
www.kjhw.de

Die Hallen sind der Funktion entsprechend unterschiedlich gestaltet, wobei sie zusammen ein harmonisches Ensemble bilden. So sind die Proportionen der Architekturelemente sowie Materialien und Farben einheitlich und zurückhaltend konzipiert, wodurch ein angemessener Rahmen für Ausstellungen entstand.

The exhibition halls are structured differently, depending on their uses, but together, they create a harmonious ensemble. In this way, proportions of the architectural elements, materials and colors are uniform and restrained in design terms and this means an appropriate context has been created for exhibitions.

Les salles sont conçues différemment en fonction de leur utilisation et pourtant elles forment un ensemble harmonieux. Les proportions des éléments architecturaux ainsi que les matériaux et couleurs sont homogènes et discrets favorisant ainsi un cadre adapté aux expositions.

Las naves están configuradas de manera distinta según su función a lo cual forman juntas un conjunto armonioso. Así, las proporciones de los elementos de la arquitectura así como los materiales y los colores están planeados de forma uniforme y discreta con lo que surgió un marco adecuado para las exposiciones.

Bundesgartenschau 2005

Federal Garden Show

Rainer Schmidt Landschaftsarchitekten

2005
Messestadt Riem

www.buga05.de
www.schmidt-landschaftsarchitekten.de

Der „Perspektivenwechsel", der Wechsel zwischen Groß und Klein, ist gestalterisches Thema im gesamten BUGA-Gelände. Die Ausstellungsbereiche konzentrieren sich auf ein Areal, das im Anschluss der Schau mit Wohnhäusern bebaut wird. Die Entstehung eines neuen Stadtteils soll hier nachhaltig sichtbar gemacht werden.

The "changing perspectives", the switch from large to small-scale, is the design theme for the Federal Garden Show (BUGA) site. Exhibition areas are concentrated to an areal zone, which will be used to build homes immediately after the show has finished. A new city precinct is to be created here, which will be made visible by degrees.

Le changement de perspective, l'alternance entre grand et petit, est un thème conceptuel présent sur tout l'espace de l'exposition nationale d'horticulture (BUGA). Les zones d'exposition se concentrent sur un terrain où des maisons d'habitation seront construites après l'exposition. La création d'un nouveau quartier urbain doit être rendue visible de manière durable.

El "cambio de perspectivas", el cambio entre grande y pequeño, es el tema del diseño en todo el recinto de la Feria Federal de Jardinería (BUGA). Las zonas de exposiciones se concentran en un área que, a continuación de la feria, es edificada con viviendas. El levantamiento de un nuevo barrio ha de hacerse visible aquí de forma duradera.

Bauzentrum München

Building Center

Hild und K Architekten
Haumann und Fuchs (SE)

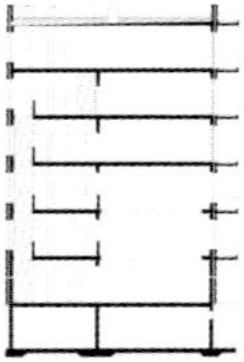

2003
Willy-Brandt-Allee 10
Messestadt Riem

www.hildundk.de

Im Bauzentrum können Firmen sich und ihre Produkte dauerhaft präsentieren. Es ist in Stahlbeton-Fertigbauweise errichtet, wobei alle Oberflächen unbehandelt sind und den Fertigungsprozess zeigen. Die Fassade wirkt wie eine Aufeinanderstapelung von großen, aneinander gereihten Schaufenstern.

In the building center, companies have a permanent exhibition space for their firm and products. It is constructed by ready-made steel concrete structure, with all surfaces remaining untreated to show the production process. The façade looks like a series of large display windows, stacked on top of each other and ordered next to each other in rows.

Dans le centre architectural, les sociétés et leurs produits peuvent se présenter de manière durable. C'est une construction en béton armé préfabriqué dans laquelle toutes les surfaces sont restées brutes et révèlent le processus de fabrication. La façade semble être un empilage de grandes vitrines alignées les unes à côté des autres.

En el centro de construcciones pueden presentarse las empresas y sus productos de forma duradera. Está erigido como una construcción prefabricada de hormigón armado a lo cual todas las superficies están sin tratar mostrando el proceso de fabricación. La fachada parece un apilado de grandes escaparates puestos en fila.

to stay . hotels

Hotel Cortiina

Albert Weinzierl

2001
Ledererstraße 8
Altstadt

www.cortiina.com

Eine Wohlfühloase. Für die Inneneinrichtung verwendete man fast ausschließlich natürliche Materialien wie Eichenparkett, Mooreichenwände und im Bad hellen Jura-Naturstein. Tagsüber ist das Hotel optimaler Ausgangspunkt für Sightseeing-Touren, abends dient der Speisesaal als Lounge.

This is a feel-good oasis. Natural materials, such as oak parquet, moor oak walls and light, natural Jura stone in the bathroom, were almost exclusively used for interior furnishing. During the day, the hotel is an optimal starting point for sightseeing tours. In the evening, the dining hall serves as a lounge.

Une oasis de bien-être. Pour l'aménagement intérieur, on a utilisé presque exclusivement des matériaux naturels comme du parquet en chêne, des murs en chêne fossile et, pour la salle de bains, de la pierre naturelle du Jura. Pendant la journée, l'hôtel est le point de départ des visites organisées des environs, et le soir, la salle de restauration sert de salon-bar.

Un oasis de placer. Para la decoración interior se utilizaron casi exclusivamente los materiales naturales como el parquet de roble, las paredes de roble negro en el baño y la piedra natural clara jurásica. Durante el día el hotel es un punto de partida óptimo para los circuitos turísticos, por las noches el comedor sirve de lounge.

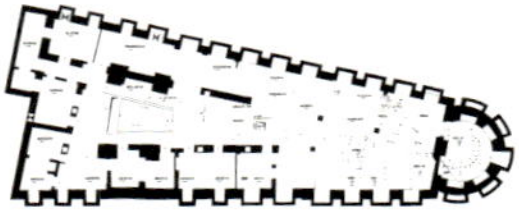

Hotel Anna

Atelier Dahms

2002
Schützenstraße 1
Ludwigsvorstadt-Isarvorstadt

www.annahotel.de

Das Anna Hotel ist als eines der 100 besten Designhotels Europas ausgezeichnet worden. Die Innenräume sind minimalistisch gestaltet, auf pompöses Interieur und übertriebenen Luxus wurde verzichtet. Das Herz des Hotels bildet sein Restaurant mit seiner eindrucksvollen wechselnden Beleuchtung.

The Hotel Anna has been distinguished as one of Europe's 100 best design hotels. The interior design is minimalist and pompous style and exaggerated luxury were avoided. The restaurant forms the heart of the hotel with its impressive, changing lighting.

L'hôtel Anna a été sélectionné comme l'un des 100 meilleurs hôtels de design d'Europe. Les espaces intérieurs sont conçus de manière minimale, le style pompeux et le luxe exagéré ont été bannis. Le cœur de l'hôtel est un restaurant pourvu d'un éclairage changeant spectaculaire.

El Hotel Anna ha sido distinguido como uno de lo 100 mejores hoteles de diseño de Europa. Los interiores están configurados de forma minimalista habiéndose renunciado a un interior pomposo y un lujo exagerado. El corazón del hotel lo constituye su restaurante con su impresionante iluminación cambiante.

Hotel Dorint Sofitel Bayerpost

Klein Haller – k/h Büro für Innenarchitektur und Design

2004
Bayerstraße 12
Ludwigsvorstadt-Isarvorstadt

www.dorint.de
www.klein-haller.de

Hinter einer geschichtsträchtigen Fassade verbirgt sich eine der modernsten Innenraumgestaltungen, die in einem bühnenähnlichen Lichtkonzept gipfelt. Die Gästezimmer greifen alpenländische Motive auf, sind reduziert gestaltet, wobei natürliche Materialien und ruhige Farben eine entspannende Wirkung ausüben.

One of the most modern interior design concepts, which culminates in a stage-like lighting concept, is concealed behind a historically significant façade. Guest rooms adopt Alpine landscape motifs, designed with reduction, with natural materials and tranquil colors exerting a relaxing effect.

Derrière une façade porteuse d'histoire se cache une conception d'intérieur extrêmement moderne qui atteint son point culminant dans un concept lumineux de scène. Les chambres d'hôte reprennent des motifs alpins, elles sont de conception minimale et les matériaux naturels associés à des couleurs douces créent une atmosphère détendue.

Detrás de una fachada cargada de historia se oculta uno de los diseños de interiores más modernos que corona en un plan de iluminación similar al de un escenario. Las habitaciones retoman motivos alpinos, están diseñadas de forma reducida a lo cual los materiales naturales y los colores tranquilos ejercen un efecto relajante.

Hotel Advokat

Kevin Voigt

1996
Baaderstraße 1
Ludwigsvorstadt-Isarvorstadt

www.hotel-advokat.de

Münchens allererstes Designhotel präsentiert sich unaufdringlich trendig. Kunst und Design sind die Hauptdarsteller. Übers ganze Haus verteilte Büsten, Gemälde, Blumenarrangements sowie ausgesuchtes Mobiliar und Lichtspiele zeugen von der Lust des Besitzers Kevin Voigt am Gestalten.

Munich's very first design hotel introduces itself in a low-key and trendy fashion. Art and design are the main illustrators. Busts, paintings, flower arrangements as well as specially selected furnishing are scattered through the hotel and light plays show the owner's, Kevin Voigt's love of design.

Le tout premier hôtel de design de Munich affiche un modernisme discret. L'art et le design sont les acteurs principaux. Des bustes et des peintures, des compositions florales ainsi qu'un mobilier recherché et des effets de lumière illustrent bien le goût du propriétaire Kevin Voigt pour la conception artistique.

El primer hotel de diseño de Munich se presenta a la moda de forma discreta. El arte y el diseño son los actores principales. Los bustos, las pinturas y los arreglos florales distribuidos por toda la casa así como el mobiliario escogido y los juegos de luces dan testimonio del gusto del propietario, Kevin Vogt, por el diseño.

Cosmopolitan Hotel

Atelier Dahms

1995
Hohenzollernstraße 5
Schwabing

www.cosmopolitan-hotel.de

Mitten in Schwabing präsentiert sich das Hotel als ein Haus, das einerseits durch klare Funktionalität und Vielseitigkeit besticht, anderseits von warmen Naturmaterialien geprägt wird. Die Innengestaltung wurde von den Designern dazu ebenso zeitlos wie konsequent mit Möbeln von Ligne Roset eingerichtet.

In central Schwabing, the hotel presents itself as a building that is striking in one sense for its clear functionality and variety and in another sense for the influence of warm and natural materials. The designers also used interior design that is as timeless as consistent with the choice of furniture by Ligne Roset.

Situé au centre de Schwabing, cet hôtel séduit, d'une part, par sa fonctionnalité et sa diversité, et d'autre part, par ses matériaux naturels chauds. Le design intérieur a été conçu de manière intemporelle avec des meubles de la Ligne Roset.

El hotel se presenta en el centro de Schwabing como una casa que, por un lado, cautiva por su clara funcionalidad y su variedad y, por otro lado, está marcada por los materiales cálidos naturales. Además, la configuración interior fue instalada por los diseñadores de forma tan intemporal como consecuente con los muebles de Ligne Roset.

Dorint Novotel München Messe

Allmann Sattler Wappner Architekten
Tombusch & Brumann

2004
Willy-Brandt-Platz 1
Messestadt Riem

www.dorint.de
www.tombusch-brumann.de
www.allmannsattlerwappner.de

Das Hotel liegt inmitten des neuen Stadtteils Messestadt Riem. Es zeichnet sich durch lichte Raumgestaltung, helle Farben und die Verwendung von hochwertigen Materialien wie Naturholz, Keramik, Stahl und satiniertes Glas aus. Farbige Akzente und dezente Lichtquellen tragen zu einer warmen modernen Atmosphäre bei.

The hotel is located right in the center of the new city district of Messestadt Riem. It is characterized by light room design, bright colors and the use of high quality materials, such as natural wood, ceramics, steel and satined glass. Colorful notes and subtle light sources contribute to a warm, modern atmosphere.

L'hôtel se situe au plein centre du nouveau quartier de la Messestadt Riem. Il se caractérise par sa conception intérieure lumineuse, ses couleurs claires et l'utilisation de matériaux de haute qualité comme le bois naturel, la céramique, l'acier et le verre satiné. Des accents de couleur et des sources lumineuses discrètes contribuent à créer une atmosphère moderne et chaleureuse.

El hotel se encuentra en medio del nuevo barrio de Messestadt Riem. Se caracteriza por una configuración del espacio luminosa, los colores claros y el empleo de materiales de alta calidad como la madera natural, la cerámica, el acero y el vidrio satinado. Los acentos de color y las fuentes de luz discretas contribuyen a una atmósfera cálida y moderna.

Kempinski Hotel Airport München

Murphy / Jahn

1994
Terminalstraße Mitte 20
Freising-Erding

www.kempinski-airport.de
www.murphyjahn.com

Das Kempinski Hotel ist von Stararchitekt Helmut Jahn entworfen worden und ist Europas modernstes Flughafenhotel. Die lichte Konstruktion ist von weitem zu erkennen, ein Palmenhain in der hohen, gläsernen Eingangshalle bildet einen an Urlaub erinnernden Blickfang in der funktionalen Umgebung des Flughafens.

The Kempinski Hotel was designed by star architect Helmut Jahn and is Europe's most modern airport hotel. The light construction can be seen from a distance, a palm grove in the tall, glass entrance hall forms an eye-catching zone reminiscient of holidays, but in the functional surroundings of the airport.

L'hôtel Kempinski a été conçu par l'architecte culte Helmut Jahn. C'est l'hôtel d'aéroport le plus moderne d'Europe. La construction lumineuse se reconnaît de loin, une haie de palmiers plantés dans le hall de réception en verre ajoute une ambiance de vacances dans l'environnement fonctionnel de l'aéroport.

El Hotel Kempinski ha sido proyectado por el arquitecto estrella Helmut Jahn y es el hotel de aeropuerto más moderno de Europa. La construcción luminosa puede reconocerse desde lejos, un campo de palmeras en el alto vestíbulo de entrada acristalado constituye un blanco de las miradas y recuerda a las vacaciones dentro del entorno funcional del aeropuerto.

HOTEL

to go . eating
drinking
clubbing
leisure
wellness, beauty & sport

Bar Comercial

Stadler + Partner Architekten

2003
Fünf Höfe
Theatinerstraße 16
Altstadt

www.planungswelt.de

Im „Comercial" blieben die Decke und der Putz unverkleidet. Im Kontrast dazu stehen die beim Ausbau verwendeten Materialien: Eiche, Stahl und Leder, ein speziell bedruckter Stoff als Wandbespannung. Eine atmosphärische Beleuchtung passt sich den wechselnden Lichtverhältnissen bei Tag und Nacht an.

The ceiling and plaster-work were left untreated in the "Comercial". The materials used in the redevelopment are a contrast: oak, steel, leather and a specially printed material as a wall covering. Atmospheric lighting can be altered to suit changing light conditions at day and night.

Le plafond et le crépi du « Comercial » sont restés à nu. Ils contrastent avec les matériaux utilisés pour l'aménagement : chêne, acier et cuir, un tissu à l'imprimé spécial recouvre les murs. Un éclairage d'ambiance s'adapte jour et nuit aux changements de lumière.

En el "Comercial" los techos y el revoque quedaron sin revestir. Con ello contrastan los materiales utilizados en la ampliación: el roble, el acero y el cuero, un tejido estampado especialmente como revestimiento. Una iluminación atmosférica se adapta a las condiciones de luz cambiantes durante el día y la noche.

Emporio Armani Caffè

In-house architects Giorgio Armani

2003
Fünf Höfe
Theatinerstraße 12
Altstadt

www.emporioarmani.com

Oberhalb des Armani Store liegt das „Emporio Armani Caffè“, ein Lokal mit Restaurant samt Bar. Im Barbereich dominiert eine farblich illuminierte Theke, die im Kontrast steht zu den sonst verwendeten Materialien: dunkle Hölzer, Punktstrahler und warme Wollstoffe als Sitzbezug.

The “Emporio Armani Caffè” is located above the Armani Store. It is a facility with restaurant and bar. In the bar area, a colorfully illuminated reception dominates and is a contrast to the materials that are used elsewhere: dark woods, spot-lighting and warm woollen materials as seat covers.

Au-dessus du magasin Armani se trouve le local « Emporio Armani Caffè » avec son restaurant et son bar. Dans le coin bar, un comptoir coloré et lumineux constraste avec les autres matériaux utilisés : du bois sombre, des spots et des étoffes chaudes pour les sièges.

Sobre el Armani Store está situado el “Emporio Armani Caffè”, un local con restaurante y bar incluido. En el recinto del bar domina un mostrador iluminado en color que está en contraste con los otros materiales utilizados: las maderas oscuras, los proyectores puntuales y los cálidos materiales de lana como fundas de los asientos.

Brasserie Leon

Dörken + Partner Innenarchitektur

2003
Bayerstraße 3-5
Ludwigsvorstadt-Isarvorstadt

www.leons.org

Das Restaurant im neuen Mathäser Filmpalast besticht durch schlichte Linien und warme Farbflächen, die dem Raum eine Atmosphäre von Ruhe und Modernität geben. Den zentralen Bereich bildet ein Kubus aus zwei Beton- und zwei Glaswänden, der an einen japanischen Zen-Garten erinnert.

The restaurant in the new Mathäser Filmpalast is striking for its simple lines and warm-colored surfaces, which give the room an atmosphere of calm and modernity. The central area forms a cube of two concrete and two glass walls, which are reminiscent of a Japanese Zen garden.

Le restaurant situé dans le Mathäser Filmpalast séduit par ses lignes sobres et ses surfaces de couleur chaudes qui donnent à la pièce une atmosphère calme et contemporaine. La zone centrale formant un cube constitué de deux murs en béton et de deux murs en verre rappelle un jardin zen japonais.

El restaurante en el nuevo Mathäser Filmpalast cautiva con las líneas sencillas y las cálidas superficies de color que otorgan al espacio una atmósfera de tranquilidad y modernidad. Un cubo de dos paredes de vidrio y dos de hormigón que recuerda a un jardín japonés del Zen forma el área central.

Nero pizza & lounge

Landau + Kindelbacher Architekten – Innenarchitekten

2004
Rumfordstraße 34
Ludwigsvorstadt-Isarvorstadt

www.nero-muenchen.de
www.landaukindelbacher.de

Nero besteht aus einem zweigeschossigen Gastraum mit Galerie. Eine von hinten beleuchtete Glassplitterwand aus grünem Recycling Glas gliedert die 8 Meter hohe Stirnseite und flutet den Raum mit atmosphärischem Licht. Hängende Lichtkugeln aus weißem Kunststoff erzeugen eine stimmungsvolle Raumbeleuchtung.

Nero is a guest room on two levels with gallery. A glass splinter wall of green recycled glass, with back-lighting, forms the 8 meter tall front side and floods the room with atmospheric light. Suspended light spheres of white plastic produce atmospheric lighting in the room.

Nero se compose d'une salle sur deux étages avec galerie. Un mur d'éclats de verre recyclés de couleur verte, illuminé par l'arrière, structure la partie frontale de 8 mètres de haut et déverse une lumière particulière dans l'espace. Des boules lumineuses suspendues, en matière synthétique blanche, contribuent à créer une lumière d'ambiance.

El Nero consta de un comedor de dos plantas con una galería. Una pared de astillas de vidrio iluminada por detrás y hecha de vidrio verde reciclado divide el frente de 8 metros de altura e inunda el espacio de luz atmosférica. Unas bolas de luz colgantes de material artificial blanco producen una iluminación interior de gran ambiente.

Cocoon

Viscons

2003
Christophstraße 3
Lehel

www.go-cocoon.de
www.viscons.com

Eine auffallende Lichtwand dominiert die Inneneinrichtung in hellen, gebrochenen Cremefarben. Mal taucht sie alles in Ozeanblau, mal sorgt Rubinrot für eine gedämpfte Atmosphäre. Der Kontrast zwischen dem weichen und neutralen Interieur und dem passenden Licht gibt dem cocoon eine moderne und stylische Atmosphäre.

A striking, light wall dominates the interior furnishing in light, broken cream colors. Occasionally, it floods everything in ocean blue, occasionally, ruby red ensures a subdued atmosphere. The contrast between the soft and neutral interior and appropriate lighting gives the cocoon a modern and stylish atmosphere.

Une paroi de lumière intense domine l'aménagement intérieur conçu en tons crème dégradés. Cette lumière plonge l'endroit dans un bleu océan ou un rouge rubis, ce dernier assurant une ambiance feutrée. Le contraste entre l'intérieur souple et neutre et la lumière du moment donne au cocoon une ambiance moderne d'un style particulier.

Una pared de luz que llama la atención domina el diseño interior en colores crema claros y apagados. Unas veces lo sumerge todo en azul marino, otras veces el rojo rubí proporciona una atmósfera apagada. El contraste entre el interior suave y neutral y una luz apropiada otorga al cocoon una atmósfera moderna y con estilo.

Brenner - Grill Pasta Bar

Albert Weinzierl

2003
Maximilianstraße 15
Altstadt

www.brennergrill.de

In den Maximilianshöfen unter dem Kreuzgewölbe befindet sich im ehemaligen fürstlichen Pferdestall der Brenner Grill. Man fühlt sich hier wie in der Gesindeküche eines Gutshofes. Eine archaische Feuerstelle und schmiedeeiserne Leuchter vermitteln Geborgenheit. Das Feuerholz ist in den raumhohen Glasfenstern gestapelt.

The Brenner Grill is located in the Maximilianhöfe beneath the cross vaults, on the site of what used to be the royal stables. You feel as though you are in the servants' kitchen of an estate's courtyard here. A sense of security is conveyed by an archaic fireplace and cast iron lights. The firewood is piled up in the glass windows that are the height of the room.

Le Brenner Grill se trouve sous les voûtes en crête du Maximilianhöfe, dans une ancienne écurie princière. On se sent ici comme dans la cuisine d'une ferme. Un foyer de cheminée archaïque et des lampes en fer forgé contribuent à donner une sensation de sécurité. Le bois pour le feu est empilé dans les hautes fenêtres.

En Maximilianhöfe bajo las bóvedas de crucería se encuentra el Brenner Grill en el antiguo establo de los príncipes. Aquí uno se siente como en la cocina de una finca para la servidumbre. Un brasero arcaico y unas luces de hierro forjado transmiten recogimiento. La leña está apilada en las ventanas de cristal de la altura de la habitación.

8 Seasons

Mila Touchton

2004
Maximilianstraße 2
Altstadt

www.8-seasons.com

Die ehemalige Telekom-Kantine im vierten Stock des Postgebäudes an der Maximillianstraße wurde in eine In-Location verwandelt. Highlight ist die große Dachterrasse mit Blick auf die Türme der Frauenkirche. Der Name des Clubs geht auf den auf zwei Jahre, also acht Jahreszeiten, befristeten Mietvertrag zurück.

The former Telecom canteen on the fourth floor of the postal building on Maximillianstraße was transformed into an "in" location. The highlight is the large roof terrace with a view towards the towers of the Frauenkirche church. The name of the club is a reference to the two years, or eight seasons, which is the length of the rental contract.

Dans la Maximilianstraße, l'ancienne cantine de Telekom située au quatrième étage du bâtiment de la poste a été transformée en un endroit recherché. Le point fort est la grande terrasse du toit avec vue sur les tours de la Frauenkirche. Le nom du club provient du contrat de location conclu pour deux ans et donc huit saisons.

La antigua cantina de la Telekom en el cuarto piso del edificio de Correos en la Maximillianstraße fue transformada en un emplazamiento de moda. El punto álgido es la gran terraza en el ático con vistas a las torres de la Frauenkirche. El nombre del club se remonta al contrato de alquiler limitado a dos años, o sea a ocho estaciones.

Schumann's Bar am Hofgarten

Boesel Benkert Hohberg Architekten

2003
Odeonsplatz 6-7
Altstadt

www.schumanns.de
www.boesel-benkert-hohberg.de

Kirchheimer Muschelkalk, Serpentin, Nussbaum – an edlen Materialien wurde nicht gespart. Den hohen Raum mit den cremefarben gespachtelten Wänden dominiert eine dunkelgrüne Natursteinwand aus Serpentin. Die Tresenverkleidung, ebenfalls aus Serpentin, bildet einen Kontrast zu den gedämpft roten Lederhockern.

No savings were made on luxury materials, – shell limestone from Kirchheim, serpentine, nut wood. The high room with the cream-colored, primed walls dominates a natural stone wall that is dark green and made of serpentine. The cladding for the bar, also of serpentine, forms a contrast to the subdued red color of the leather bar stools.

Les matériaux nobles tels que le calcaire coquillier de Kirchheim, la serpentine, le noisetier ont généreusement été utilisés. La haute pièce aux parois crépies de couleur crème domine un mur de pierre naturelle vert foncé en serpentine. L'habillage du comptoir, également en serpentine, contraste avec les tabourets discrets en cuir rouge.

La caliza de conchas de Kirchheim, la serpentina, el nogal –no se ahorró en materiales nobles. Una pared de piedra natural de serpentina verde oscura domina la sala alta con las paredes alisadas en colores crema. El revestimiento del mostrador, igualmente de serpentina, forma un contraste con los taburetes de cuero de color rojo apagado.

Nektar

Patrick Ferrier

2003
Stubenvollstraße 1
Haidhausen

www.nektar.de
www.ferrierinterior.com

Das Nektar in den Gewölben des alten Preysingkellers besteht aus mehreren durchgestalteten Räumen. Das in Weiß gehaltene Tonnengewölbe mit seinen Liegeflächen kann durch wechselnde Illuminierung in unterschiedliche Farben gehüllt werden. Der Salon Orange zeichnet sich durch retro-futuristische Elemente aus.

The Nektar in the caves of the old Preysingkeller consists of several designed rooms. The barrel-vault with storage space is kept in white and can be concealed by changing lighting in different colors. The orange salon is characterized by retro and futuristic elements.

Le Nektar logé dans la Preysingkeller se compose de plusieurs pièces aux designs différents. La voûte est restée blanche mais peut être illuminée de couleurs variées. Le Salon Orange se caractérise par des éléments rétro-futuristes.

El Nektar, en las bóvedas del viejo Preysingkeller consta de varias habitaciones totalmente diseñadas. La bóveda blanca de cañón con su superficie abatible puede cubrirse de diferentes colores por medio de la iluminación cambiante. El salón Orange se caracteriza por los elementos retro-futuristas.

Falk's Bar

Sigwart Graf Pilati

2002
Promenadeplatz 2-6
Altstadt

www.bayerischerhof.de

Die Geschichte des Saales im Bayerischen Hof reicht bis ins Jahr 1841 zurück. So dominieren stuckverzierte Decken und Wände. Hauptblickfang ist der Glastresen einer von allen Seiten zugänglichen Bar, die sich in vielfältigen Farben indirekt beleuchten lässt.

The history of the room at the Bayerischer Hof dates back to 1841. This is why the walls and ceilings with stucco decoration are predominant. The main focus of attention is the glass top of a bar that can be accessed from all sides and illuminated indirectly in many different colors.

L'histoire de la salle du Bayerischer Hof remonte à l'année 1841. Les plafonds et les murs en stuc ont un caractère dominant. Le regard est accroché par le comptoir en verre du bar accessible par tous les côtés et s'illuminant de couleurs variées grâce à un éclairage indirect.

La historia de la sala en el Bayerischer Hof se remonta al año 1841. Así dominan los techos y las paredes adornadas con estuco. El principal centro de atención es el mostrador de vidrio de un bar accesible por todos los lados que puede iluminarse indirectamente en colores variados.

Lounge$_2$

Schmidhuber + Partner

2003
Bayerstraße 3-5
Ludwigsvorstadt-Isarvorstadt

www.l-lounge2.de
www.schmidhuber.de

Die Lounge ist ein bisher einmaliges Projekt, bei dem die Corporate Identity eines Wirtschaftsunternehmens auf die Gastronomie übertragen werden sollte. Die blauen Wasserblasen des Netzbetreibers O_2 sind in einer Glaswand verbildlicht, die Räume nach Unternehmens-Richtlinien jung, modern und kosmopolitisch gestaltet.

Until now, the Lounge has been a unique project that was created from the transferral of a firm's corporate identity to gastronomy. The blue bubbles of mobile telephone provider O_2 are depicted in a glass wall and the rooms are designed, according to the company's guidelines, in a young, modern and cosmopolitan style.

Le salon-bar est un projet unique dans lequel l'identité visuelle d'une entreprise économique devait être transférée à la gastronomie. Les bulles d'eau bleue de l'opérateur de réseau O_2 sont visualisées dans un mur en verre les pièces sont conçues selon l'image de l'entreprise, de manière jeune, moderne et cosmopolite.

El Lounge es un proyecto único hasta ahora en el cual la Corporate Identity de una empresa de economía había de transferirse a la gastronomía. Las burbujas azules de agua del operador de red O_2 están ilustradas en una pared de vidrio, las salas están configuradas de forma joven, moderna y cosmopolita según las directrices de la empresa.

Spa Lagune

Hotel Dorint Sofitel Bayerpost

Klein Haller – k/h Büro für Innenarchitektur und Design

2004
Bayerstraße 12
Ludwigsvorstadt-Isarvorstadt

www.dorint.de
www.klein-haller.de

Das Spa im Dorint Bayerpost erstreckt sich über fast 600 Quadratmeter. Eine geschwungene Formensprache im spiralförmig angelegten Schwimmbereich mit einem überdimensionalen Whirlpool, natürliche Materialien, weiches Licht und aromatische Düfte tun ein Übriges, um den Gast in eine andere Welt eintauchen zu lassen.

The Spa in the Bayerpost Dorint takes up almost 600 square meters. A rolling form language in a spiral-shaped swimming area with an over-sized whirlpool, natural materials, soft light and aromatic scents do the utmost to immerse the guest in another world.

Les thermes de Dorint Bayerpost s'étendent sur presque 600 mètres carrés. Le langage des formes en spirale de la zone aquatique et le bain à remous surdimensionné, ainsi que les matériaux naturels accompagnés d'une lumière douce et de senteurs aromatiques, contribuent à plonger le visiteur dans un autre monde.

El spa en el Dorint Bayerpost se extiende por casi 600 metros cuadrados. Un lenguaje de formas oscilante en el recinto de la piscina, trazado en forma de espiral, con una bañera de hidromasaje gigantesca, los materiales naturales, la luz suave y los olores aromáticos hacen el resto para que el cliente se sumerja en otro mundo.

MOVIE'S
Kino Bar Restaurant Café

Cinema Bar Restaurant Café

Anne Batisweiler

2002
Goetheplatz 2
Sendling

www.anne.batisweiler.de

Das Professor-Sep-Ruf-Gebäude am Goetheplatz wurde wieder seiner ursprünglichen Nutzung als Kino samt Gastronomie zugeführt. Die orthogonalen Räume werden verschiedenfarbig beleuchtet, die zentrale Foyererweiterung betont zudem das Zusammenspiel zwischen Kinosälen und Gastronomie.

The Professor Sep Ruf building on Goetheplatz was returned to its original purpose as a cinema with restaurant facility. The orthogonal rooms are illuminated in different colors, the central extension of the foyer also emphasizes the interplay of cinema theaters and gastronomy.

Le bâtiment du professeur Sep Ruf de la Goetheplatz a retrouvé son usage traditionnel de cinéma avec restauration. Les pièces orthogonales sont éclairées de différentes couleurs, l'agrandissement du foyer central souligne le lien entre les salles de cinéma et la gastronomie.

El edificio "Profesor Sep Ruf" en la Goetheplatz fue destinado de nuevo a su utilización original de cine junto con gastronomía. Las salas ortogonales se alumbran en colores distintos, la ampliación central del vestíbulo acentúa además la conjunción de las salas de cines con la gastronomía.

Fabien K Espace Beauté

Björn-Uwe Rosenow

2002
Utzschneiderstraße 2
Altstadt

www.fabienk.de

Der Coiffeur-Salon erfüllt den selbst gestellten Anspruch „espace beauté" mit Bravour. Die einzelnen funktionalen Zonen unterscheiden sich in Möblierung und Stimmung. Zurückhaltende Farbgestaltung, natürliche Materialien vermitteln so elegant-französisches Flair und entziehen sich dem städtischen Umfeld.

The hairdressing salon earns full marks for meeting its own requirement for "espace beauté". The individual functional zones differ in furnishing and atmosphere. Restrained use of color, natural materials transmit such an elegant, French flair and create a retreat from the urban environment.

Le salon de coiffure répond avec brio aux exigences de l'espace-beauté. Chaque zone fonctionnelle se caractérise par son mobilier et son ambiance particulière. Une conception discrète des couleurs, des matériaux naturels contribuent à donner une atmosphère française qui fait oublier l'environnement urbain.

El salón de peluquería cumple la exigencia impuesta por él mismo de ser un "espace beauté" con brillantez. Cada una de las zonas funcionales se diferencia en el amueblado y el ambiente. Así, una configuración de color discreta y unos materiales naturales transmiten un elegante encanto francés que rehuye al entorno urbano.

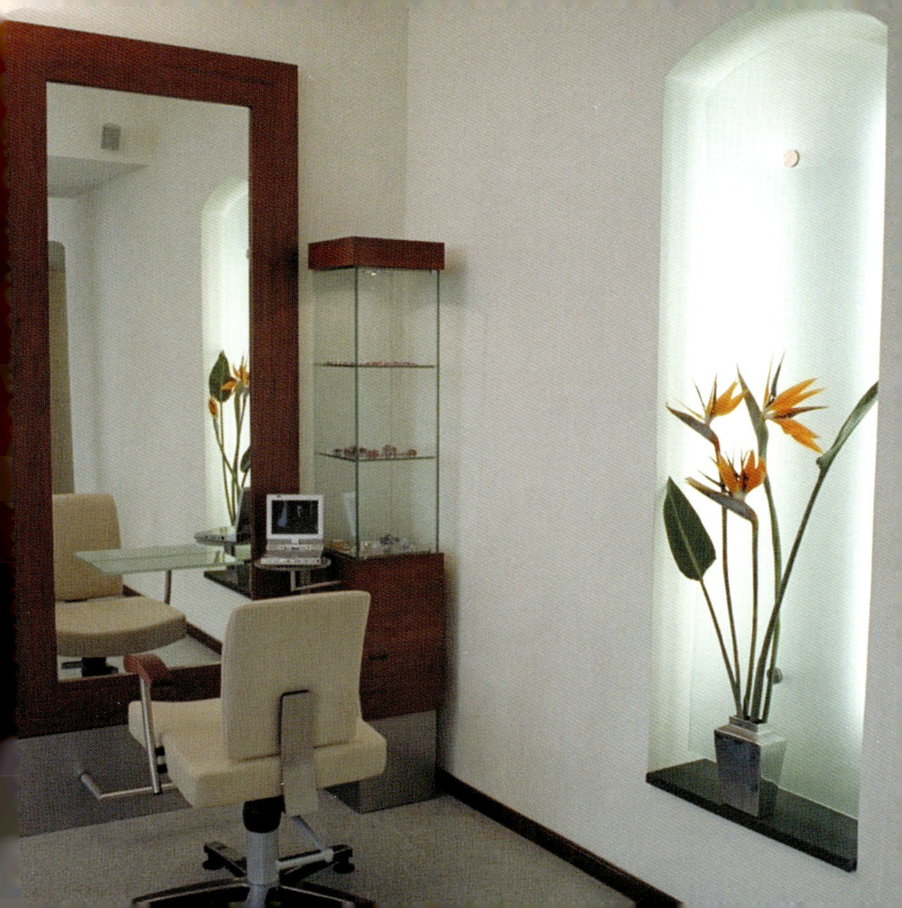

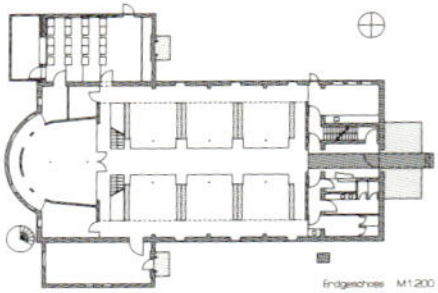

Umbau einer Kirche Einbau eines Kinos

Redevelopment of a Church into a Cinema

Stadler + Partner Architekten

2000
Schwere-Reiter-Straße 35 / 17
Schwabing

www.planungswelt.de

Die Kapelle steht auf einem ehemaligen Kasernengelände, das neu bebaut wird. Zwischenzeitlich werden die bestehenden Gebäude samt Kapelle umgenutzt. Der Einsatz kostengünstiger Materialien wie roher Stahl, Glas und Holz unterstreicht die zeitlich begrenzte Umnutzung als Büro und Kino. Von außen blieb der sakrale Charakter erhalten.

The chapel is located on the site of a former army barracks, which is being redeveloped. Meanwhile, the existing buildings, including the chapel, are reused for other things. The input of cost-effective materials such as raw steel, glass and wood underlines the limited time-scale for the redevelopment as office space and a cinema. From the outside, the religious character is to be preserved.

La chapelle se situe sur le terrain d'une ancienne caserne où de nouvelles constructions verront le jour. Entre-temps, les bâtiments existants et la chapelle sont utilisés de manière différente. Les matériaux peu coûteux comme l'acier brut, le verre et le bois renforcent l'aspect temporaire de la transformation en bureau et cinéma. De l'extérieur, le caractère sacré demeure.

La capilla está situada sobre el terreno de un antiguo cuartel que está siendo edificado nuevo. Entretanto se reaprovechan los edificios existentes incluyendo la capilla. El empleo de materiales a buen precio como el acero en bruto, el vidrio y la madera resalta la reutilización, temporalmente limitada, en oficina y cine. Por fuera se mantendrá el carácter sacro.

MunichGym
Sportcenter und Wellness

Kunze Seeholzer Architektur & Stadtplanung

2003
Kathi-Kobus-Straße 11
Schwabing

www.munichgym.de
www.kunze-seeholzer.de

Sandgestrahlte Sichtbetonflächen, Trennwände aus Industrieglas, schwere raumhohe Stahlblechtüren, offene Leitungsführung und durch die Decke gestanzte Stahlbeton-Treppenkerne stehen für ein Konzept, das von großer Individualität geprägt ist und sich von herkömmlichen Studioketten abhebt.

Sand-blasted exposed concrete surfaces, partition walls of industrial glass, heavy, steel panel doors as high as the room, open cable-work and a staircase of steel and reinforced concrete punched in the ceiling represent a concept that is characterized by a high level of individuality and distinguished from conventional studio chains.

Les surfaces en béton apparent sablé, les cloisons en verre industriel, les portes en tôle d'acier de la même hauteur que la pièce, les conduites visibles et l'escalier en béton armé perçant le plafond sont synonymes d'un concept empreint d'une grande individualité qui se démarque des salles de musculation habituelles.

Las superficies de hormigón liso tratadas con chorros de arena, las paredes de separación de vidrio industrial, las puertas de chapa de acero de la altura de las habitaciones, las conducciones abiertas y los núcleos de las escaleras de hormigón armado cortados a través de los techos son sinónimo de un plan marcado por un gran individualismo y que se destaca de las cadenas de gimnasios habituales.

Interimbettenhaus
in Modulbauweise
Temporary Hospital Bed Accommodation

Guggenbichler + Netzer Architekten

2001
Kölner Platz 1
Schwabing

www.guggenbichler-netzer.de

Als Ausweichquartier während der Sanierung des Krankenhauses München-Schwabing ist ein vorgefertigtes Containergebäude verwendet worden, das von Augsburg nach München umgesetzt wurde. Ein neues Treppenhaus verbindet die Ebenen und schließt an einen unterirdischen Verbindungsgang zum Altbau an.

A prefabricated container building was used as alternative accommodation during the renovation of the hospital in Munich's Schwabing district. The accommodation was moved from Augsburg to Munich. A new stairway connects the different levels and joins the old building by an underground linking passage.

Un bâtiment-container préfabriqué a été utilisé pour servir d'espace provisoire pendant la rénovation de l'hôpital München-Schwabing, qui a été transféré de Augsbourg à Munich. Un nouvel escalier relie les différents niveaux et l'entrée souterraine menant au vieux bâtiment.

Como alojamiento alternativo durante la reforma del hospital de Munich-Schwabing se utilizó un edificio de contenedores prefabricado que fue trasladado de Augsburgo a Munich. Unas escaleras nuevas unen los niveles y conectan con la edificación vieja en un paso subterráneo de conexión.

mi koo allsense-institute

Hans Panschar
Schreinerei Josef Eham

2003
Norderneyer Straße 12
Milbertshofen

www.mi-koo.com
www.hanspanschar.de
www.eham.de

mi koo allsense ist eine Hommage an fernöstliche Architektur. Das Interieur verbindet asiatisches Flair mit ökologischen Materialien und modernem Design. Durch Wände, die an Papierschiebetüren erinnern, schlichte Einbauten aus hochwertigen Holzarten, Farben und Düfte wird dieser Eindruck noch verstärkt.

mi koo allsense is an homage to far eastern architecture. The interior connects Asian flair with ecological materials and modern design. This impression is even intensified by walls that are reminiscent of paper sliding doors, simple installations of high quality wood varieties, colors and aromas.

mi koo allsense est un hommage à l'architecture d'extrême-orient. L'intérieur réunit le caractère asiatique et les matériaux écologiques avec un design moderne. Les murs rappelant des portes en papier coulissantes, les éléments dépouillés en bois précieux, les couleurs et les senteurs confirment cette impression.

El mi koo allsense es un homenaje a la arquitectura del lejano oriente. El interior une el encanto asiático con los materiales ecológicos y el diseño moderno. Esta impresión se intensifica todavía más por medio de las paredes que recuerdan a las puertas correderas de papel, de los módulos sencillos de tipos de madera de alta calidad, de los colores y los aromas.

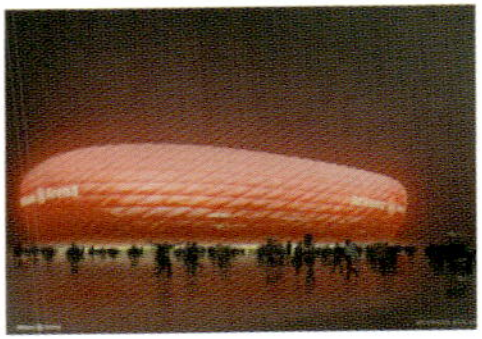

Allianz Arena

Herzog & De Meuron
SSP Sailer Stepan und Partner (SE)

2005
Werner-Heisenberg-Allee 25
Fröttmaning

www.allianz-arena.de
www.herzogdemeuron.ch

Das neue Fußballstadion besticht durch seine transluzente Umhüllung aus ETFE-Folie, die von innen in unterschiedlichen Farben beleuchtet wird und selbstreinigend ist. Je nachdem welcher Verein spielt, wird sie das Stadion in Rot, Blau oder Weiß hüllen und schon von Weitem als Wahrzeichen wirken.

The new football stadium is striking due to its translucent wrapping in ETFE foil that is illuminated from the inside in different colors and is self-cleaning. Depending on which club is playing, it covers the stadium in red, blue or white and it already looks like a landmark from a distance.

Le nouveau stade de footbal séduit grâce à son enveloppe translucide autonettoyante en plastique ETFE, éclairée de l'intérieur dans une couleur au choix. Selon le club en compéti-tion, le stade est plongé dans une lumière rouge, bleue ou blanche et l'enveloppe-emblème se reconnaît de loin.

El nuevo estadio de fútbol cautiva por su envoltura translúcida de plástico de ETFE que es iluminado por dentro en colores distintos y se autolimpia. Según el club que juegue cubrirá el estadio de rojo, azul o blanco produciendo ya desde lejos la impresión de un símbolo característico.

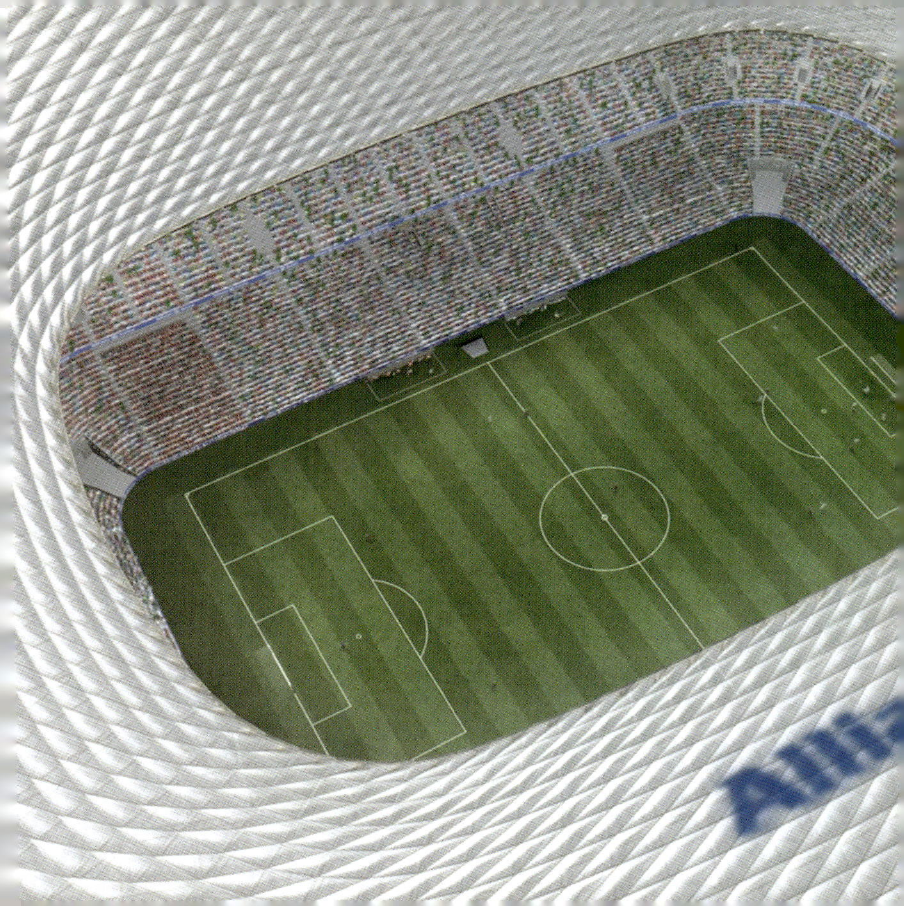

Hallenbad Westbad

Indoor Swimming Pool

RPM Architekten

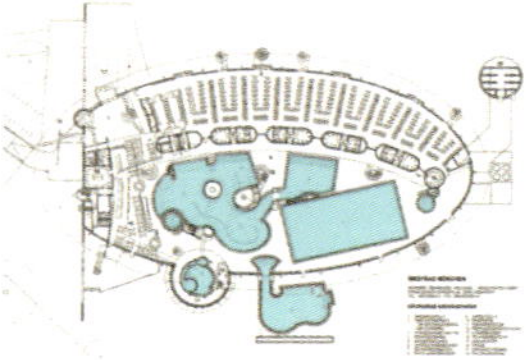

1998
Weinberger Straße 11
Pasing

www.rpm-architekten.de

Das elliptische Gebäudeensemble wirkt ruhig und trotz seiner Größe elegant und geschmeidig. Auf der einen Seite eröffnet es den Blick in den Park, auf der anderen lässt die Glaskuppel über dem Becken viel Sonne in den Innenraum und intensiviert so die Beziehung Innen und Außen.

The elliptical building ensemble looks peaceful, elegant and flexible, despite its size. On the one side, the view opens up onto the park, on the other side, the glass dome above the pool lets in lots of sunshine and in this way the relationship between inside and outside is made more intense.

Cet ensemble de bâtiments elliptiques donne une impression de calme, et malgré sa grande taille, il est élégant et souple. D'un côté, il s'ouvre vers le parc, et de l'autre, la coupole en verre surplombant le bassin laisse le soleil pénétrer dans l'espace intérieur et intensifie la relation intérieur-extérieur.

El conjunto elíptico de edificios parece tranquilo y a pesar de su tamaño elegante y suave. Por un lado abre la visión hacia el parque, por el otro la cúpula de cristal deja entrar en el interior mucho sol sobre la piscina intensificando así la relación entre el interior y el exterior.

Südbad

Indoor Swimming Pool

Guggenbichler + Netzer Architekten

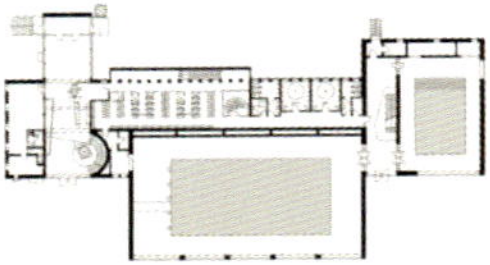

2000
Valleystraße 37
Sendling

www.guggenbichler-netzer.de

Das Bad aus den 50er Jahren wurde komplett entkernt und umgebaut. Der neue Anbau ermöglicht eine geänderte interne Erschließung. Die verwendeten Materialien wie farblich gemischte Mosaikfliesen, Betonwerkstein, starke Farbflächen und klare Formen führen die Architektur der 50er Jahre fort.

The 1950s swimming pool was completely taken apart and remodeled. The new extension makes it possible to change access routes inside. The use of materials, such as mosaic tiles in different colors, concrete building block, strong surface colors and clear forms continue the 1950s architecture.

La piscine des années 50 a été démolie puis reconstruite. La nouvelle construction permet une modification de l'organisation interne. Les matériaux utilisés tels les carreaux en mosaïque de divers coloris, les parpaings en béton, les surfaces de couleurs vives et les formes nettes reprennent l'architecture des années 50.

Los baños de los años 50 fueron retirados y reformados. La nueva ampliación hace posible una edificación interna modificada. Los materiales utilizados, como las baldosas de mosaico de colores mezclados, el bloque de hormigón, las superficies de color fuertes y las formas claras continúan la arquitectura de los años 50.

AltiraSPA - Wellness Club

ArabellaSheraton Grand Hotel

Brigitte Freyberg

2003
Arabellastraße 6
Bogenhausen

www.altiraspa.com,
www.arabellasheraton.com

Das erste Spa der neuen Wellnessmarke der ArabellaSheraton Gruppe wurde in München eröffnet. Auf einer Fläche von über 1000 Quadratmeter befinden sich ein Indoor-Pool und ein Fitness-Wintergarten. In zarten Farben von Hand bemalte Säulen und Wände geben dem Spa einen stilvollen und harmonischen Rahmen.

The first spa of the new fitness brand for the ArabellaSheraton group was opened in Munich. An indoor pool and fitness conservatory are located in an area of over 1,000 square meters. The spa has a stylish and harmonious backdrop due to the delicate colors of hand-painted columns and walls.

Les nouveaux thermes du groupe ArabellaSheraton ont été inaugurés à Munich. Une piscine couverte et un centre sportif logé dans un jardin d'hiver se partagent la surface de 1000 mètres carrés. Les couleurs des colonnes et des murs peints à la main donnent aux thermes un cadre plein de style et d'harmonie.

El primer spa de la nueva marca de wellness del grupo Arabella Sheraton fue abierto en Munich. Sobre una superficie de 1000 metros cuadrados hay una piscina interior y una terraza de invierno para fitness. Los pilares y las paredes pintados a mano en colores delicados dotan al spa de un marco armonioso y con estilo.

to shop . mall
retail
showrooms

Fünf Höfe

Herzog & De Meuron, Ivano Gianola Mendrisio, Hillmer & Sattler
OPB Obermeyer Planen + Beraten (SE), Burger + Fischer (SE)

2003
Maffeistraße, Theatinerstraße,
Kardinal-Faulhaber-Straße
Altstadt

www.fuenfhoefe.de
www.herzogdemeuron.ch
www.h-s-a.de

Als Neugestaltung eines gesamten Stadtblocks ist mit den Fünf Höfen eines der größten Innenstadtbauprojekte Deutschlands fertig gestellt worden. Historische Gebäude, moderne Architektur, abwechslungsreiche Passagen und Innenhöfe dienen der Kultur, Kommunikation, Wirtschaft, Gastronomie und dem Handel.

The Fünf Höfe (five courtyards) was a plan to redesign an entire block in the city and one of Germany's most major inner city building projects was completed. Historical buildings, modern architecture, passage-ways full of variety and inner courtyards serve culture, communication, the economy, gastronomy and trade.

La reconstruction d'un bloc de quartier complet (Fünf Höfe), l'un des plus grands projets architecturaux urbains d'Allemagne, vient de se terminer. Les bâtiments historiques, l'architecture moderne, les diverses galeries et les cours intérieures répondent aux besoins culturels et aux exigences de communication, d'économie, de restauration et de commerce.

Uno de los mayores proyectos de la arquitectura urbana en Alemania se concluyó con los Fünf Höfe (Cinco Patios) como la remodelación de un bloque urbano completo. Los edificios históricos, la arquitectura moderna, los pasajes variados y los patios interiores sirven para la cultura, comunicación, economía, gastronomía y el comercio.

Camper

Marti Guixé / Ingo Maurer

2003
Fünf Höfe
Theatinerstraße 16
Altstadt

www.camper.com
www.guixe.com
www.ingo-maurer.com

Der Eingang des kleinen Schuhgeschäftes ist etwas in eines der Gebäude der Fünf Höfe zurückversetzt. Die Einrichtung ist ein reduziertes Konzept mit Kontrasten in Farbe und Licht. Ausgeleuchtet wird der Laden durch eindrucksvolle Leuchten des Lichtkünstlers Ingo Maurer.

The entrance of the small shoe store is rather set back in one of the Fünf Höfe buildings. The interior is based on a concept of reduction, with color and light contrasts. The store's lighting is provided by the impressive lamps by lighting artist, Ingo Maurer.

L'entrée du petit magasin de chaussures a été transférée dans un des bâtiments Fünf Höfe. L'aménagement est réduit à un concept de contrastes de couleur et de lumière. Le magasin est éclairé par un arrangement lumineux exécuté par l'artiste Ingo Maurer.

La entrada al pequeño comercio de calzado está desplazada un poco hacia dentro de uno de los edificios de los Fünf Höfe. La decoración constituye un plan reducido con contrastes de color y luz. La tienda se ilumina por medio de lámparas impresionantes del artista de la luz Ingo Maurer.

Bethge

Johannes Vogelsanger

2000
Schäfflerhof
Theatinerstraße 1
Altstadt

www.bethge-hamburg.de
www.jv-architekt.de

Die Luxus-Papeterie. Schon das klare und schnörkellose Design ist extravagant: Ovale Beton-Regale, Vitrinen aus dunkler Eiche, die Decke unterteilt durch Aluminium-Elemente. Das wirkt extrem stylish, fast wie ein Wallpaper-Titel – sehr luxuriös für ein Schreibwaren-Geschäft.

The luxury stationers. The clear and unfussy design is already extravagant: oval concrete shelves, display cabinets of dark oak, the ceiling divided by aluminium elements. This all looks extremely stylish, almost like a wallpaper name—very luxurious for a stationers' store.

La papeterie de luxe. Le design net et sans fioriture est pourtant extravagant : des étagères ovales en béton, des vitrines en chêne sombre, le plafond est divisé par des éléments en aluminium. Le style obtenu fait penser au titre d'un Wallpaper, touche très luxueuse pour une papeterie.

La papelería de lujo. Ya el diseño claro y sin adornos es extravagante: las estanterías ovales de hormigón, las vitrinas de roble oscuro, el techo subdividido por elementos de aluminio. Esto produce un efecto de mucho estilo, casi como un número de Wallpaper, muy lujoso para un comercio de artículos de papelería.

Bayerischer Kunstgewerbe-Verein

Bavarian Arts-and-Crafts Club

Landau + Kindelbacher Architekten – Innenarchitekten

2000
Pacellistraße 6-8
Altstadt

www.kunsthandwerk-bkv.de
www.landaukindelbacher.de

Der Laden dient als Ausstellungsplattform für die Mitglieder des Bayerischen Kunstgewerbevereins im Bereich zeitgenössisches Kunsthandwerk und Schmuck. Eine massive Faltung aus mattiertem Glas schafft eine differenzierte räumliche Gliederung. Freie Bereiche bieten Platz für wechselnde Ausstellungen.

The shop serves as an exhibition opportunity for members of the Bavarian Arts-and-Crafts Club in the field of contemporary art handicrafts and jewelry. A massive fold of matt glass creates a differentiated spatial structure. Free areas offer space for changing exhibitions.

Le magasin sert de plateforme d'exposition pour les objets d'artisanat et les bijoux contemporains produits par les membres du club bavarois d'art décoratif. Une structure massive en verre mat plissé crée un espace différencié. Des zones libres sont disponibles pour les nouvelles expositions.

La tienda sirve de plataforma de exposiciones para los miembros de la Asociación Bávara de Artesanía en el ámbito de la artesanía contemporánea y la joyería. Un pliegue masivo de vidrio esmerilado crea una estructura del espacio diferenciada. Las áreas libres ofrecen espacio para las exposiciones cambiantes.

Designreisen

Designreisen

2004
Promenadeplatz 12
Altstadt

www.designreisen.de

Designreisen und Gerhard Meir von Le Coup präsentieren sich jetzt gemeinsam mit ihrem Style & Travel-Konzept unter einem Dach. Die frische und offene Einrichtung der kleinen und feinen Reiseboutique entstand in Kooperation mit Design & Light München sowie den Marken Kartell und Driade.

Designreisen and Gerhard Meir of Le Coup now present themselves together under one roof with their Style & Travel Concept. The fresh and open interior of the small and top-class travel boutique was created in cooperation with Design & Light München as well as the Kartell and Driade brands.

Designreisen et Gerhard Meir (Le Coup) se présentent ensemble sous le même toit avec leur concept de style & voyage. L'aménagement synonyme de fraîcheur de la petite et élégante boutique de voyage a été conçu en coopération avec Design & Light München et les marques Kartell et Driade.

Designreisen y Gerhard Meir de Le Coup se presentan ahora juntos bajo un techo con su concepción de Style & Travel. El equipamiento fresco y abierto de la pequeña y elegante boutique de viajes surgió en cooperación con Design & Light München así como con las marcas Kartell y Driade.

N
W
E
S
D
R

Verlagsbuchhandlung Liebeskind

Publishers' book store

Tredup & Hamann

2000
Klenzestraße 32
Ludwigsvorstadt-Isarvorstadt

www.liebeskind.de
www.treduphamann.com

Wunsch des Besitzers war ein Geschäft, das sich in Gestaltung und Atmosphäre von einer typischen Buchhandlung unterscheidet. Die Wände wurden nicht komplett mit Bücherregalen bedeckt, stattdessen wurden individuelle Präsentationselemente eingefügt. Den Lounge-Charakter verstärken Teppiche und bequeme Sitzgelegenheiten.

The owner's wish was for a store that differs in terms of design and atmosphere from a typical book store. The walls were not completely covered with book shelves and individual presentation units were included instead. The lounge character is emphasized by rugs and comfortable seating facilities.

Le propriétaire souhaitait un espace offrant une ambiance et un décor différents des librairies habituelles. Les étagères de livres ne couvrent pas tous les murs et des éléments individuels de présentation les remplacent. Le caractère salon-bar est renforcé par des tapis et des sièges confortables.

El deseo del propietario era un comercio que se diferenciara de una librería típica en su diseño y atmósfera. Las paredes no fueron cubiertas completamente de estanterías de libros, en lugar de ello se introdujeron elementos de presentación individuales. Las alfombras y los asientos cómodos hacen más intenso el carácter de lounge.

Max Aub
Max Aub
Der Zauberberg
hör

Oscar und Paul

Christoph Simmerl

2002
Rumfordstraße 48
Ludwigsvorstadt-Isarvorstadt

www.oscarundpaul.de

Auf 140 Quadratmetern moderner Verkaufsfläche werden nationale sowie internationale Designermarken angeboten. Das Sortiment steht für Individualität und Exklusivität, was durch die von Christoph Simmerl gestaltete Einrichtung aus Beton, Stahl und Holz unterstrichen werden soll.

National and international designer labels are on offer on 140 square meters of a modern sales' floor. The selection represents individuality and exclusivity, which is supposed to be underlined by an interior of concrete, steel and wood, designed by Christoph Simmerl.

La surface de vente moderne ce 140 mètres carrés offre des marques de designers nationaux et internationaux. L'assortiment exclusif est souligné par l'aménagement de Christoph Simmerl conçu en béton, acier et bois.

Sobre los 140 metros cuadrados de una superficie de ventas moderna se ofrecen marcas de diseño nacionales e internacionales. El surtido es un sinónimo de individualismo y exclusividad lo que ha de acentuarse por la instalación de hormigón, acero y madera diseñada por Christoph Simmerl.

smuk feine kost

Fine Foods

für alle. gestaltung von raum und gegenstand.
Matthias Gindhart (SE)

2001
Seitzstraße 13
Lehel

www.smuk.info
www.fueralle.net

Aus einem dunklen, altenglisch möblierten Teeladen ist ein heller, minimalistischer Verkaufsraum geworden. Die ursprüngliche Bausubstanz aus den 50er Jahren wurde wieder freigelegt, klare Blickbezüge und Durchblicke sind ermöglicht worden. Zentrum ist die Theke, an der die Speisen zubereitet werden.

A bright, minimalist sales room has been made out of a dark tea room with old English furnishing. The original 1950s building substance was rediscovered, clear viewing references and open views have been made possible. The center is the bar, where the food is prepared.

Le vieux et sombre magasin de thé meublé en style victorien est devenu un espace de vente minimaliste. La structure d'origine datant des années 50 a été remise en état pour permettre des échappées et des références visuelles. Le comptoir où se préparent les aliments occupe le centre du magasin.

Una oscura tienda de té con muebles ingleses antiguos se convirtió en una sala de ventas clara y minimalista. La estructura del edificio original de los años 50 fue puesta al descubierto de nuevo, se hicieron posibles las referencias visuales claras y la visión de conjunto. El centro es el mostrador en el que se preparan las comidas.

Maximilianhöfe

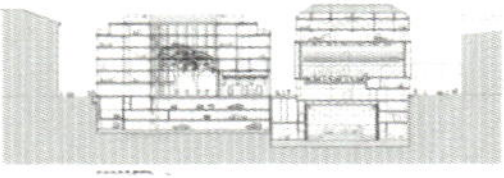

Gewers Kühn und Kühn
Hartwich / Mertens / Ingenieure (SE)

2003
Maximilianstraße 10
Altstadt

www.marstallplatz.de
www.gewers-kuehn-kuehn.de

Transparent und kommunikativ: Auf dem Marstallplatz entstehen durch die Verbindung des rekonstruierten Bürklein-Baus von 1858, dem Salpeterhof, einem neuen Operngebäude, und den verglasten sechsgeschossigen Maximilianhöfen ein neues Innenstadtzentrum für Gastronomie, Wirtschaft, Handel und Kultur.

Transparent and communicative: on Marstallplatz, the Salpeterhof, a new opera building and the glass, six storey Maximilianhöfe, a new inner-city center for gastronomy, business, trade and culture has been created by combining them with the reconstructed 1858 Bürklein building.

Transparent et communicatif : un nouveau centre urbain pour la restauration, l'économie, le commerce et la culture a été créé sur la Marstallplatz en reliant le bâtiment Bürklein de 1858 qui a été reconstruit, le Salpeterhof, le nouvel opéra et l'édifice vitré de six étages de Maximilianhöfe.

Transparentes y comunicativos: En la Marstallplatz surgen a través de la conexión del edificio Bürklein de 1858, que ha sido reconstruido, el Salpeterhof, un nuevo edificio de la ópera y los Maximilianhöfe acristalados y de seis plantas, un nuevo centro urbano para la gastronomía, la economía, el comercio y la cultura.

Valentina & me

Landau + Kindelbacher Architekten – Innenarchitekten

2004
Maximilianstraße 15
Altstadt

www.landaukindelbacher.de

Durch die offene Fensterfront wird der ganze Laden zum Schaufenster für Kinderbekleidung. Neben weißen Wänden, Lackstühlen und cremefarbenem Natursteinbelag setzen die Kleidung und das farbig veränderbare Leuchtband in der Decke Farbakzente und erwecken die Aufmerksamkeit der Passanten.

The whole shop becomes a display window for childrens' clothing because of the open window frontage. Along with white walls, lacquered chairs and cream colored natural stone surfaces, the clothes and the colorful, adjustable lighting strip in the ceiling set color tones and arouse the interest of passers-by.

La façade en verre transforme le magasin entier en vitrine dédiée à la mode enfantine. Associés aux murs blancs et au revêtement en pierre naturelle, les sièges peints, les vêtements et la bande lumineuse changeante du plafond apportent des touches de couleur et attirent l'attention des passants.

Toda la tienda se convierte en un escaparate de ropa infantil por medio de la fachada abierta de vidrio. Junto a las paredes blancas, las sillas barnizadas y el revestimiento de piedra natural de color crema, la ropa y la banda luminosa en el techo que cambia de color marcan la pauta de color y despiertan la atención de los peatones.

Mercedes-Benz Center

LAI Architekten
SSP Sailer Stepan und Partner (SE)

2002
Arnulfstraße 61-71
Neuhausen

www.muenchen.mercedes-benz.de
www.laiarchitekten.com

An einer der meistbefahrenen Verkehrsbrücken Europas bietet das transparente Gebäude optimale Präsentationsmöglichkeiten. Der komplett verglaste Baukörper wirkt wie ein überdimensionales Schaufenster und zusammen mit dem 65 Meter hohen elliptischen Glasturm markiert es den westlichen Eingang zur Innenstadt.

The transparent building offers optimal show possibilities on one of the busiest traffic bridges in Europe. The completely glass structure looks like an over-sized display window and together with the 65 meter tall, elliptical glass tower, it marks the western entrance to the city center.

Au niveau d'un des ponts routiers européens les plus utilisés d'Europe, le bâtiment transparent offre des possibilités optimales de présentation. L'édifice tout en verre ressemble à une vitrine géante, la tour elliptique en verre de 65 mètres marque l'entrée de la ville côté ouest.

Sobre uno de los puentes más transitados de Europa el edificio transparente ofrece unas posibilidades óptimas de presentación. El cuerpo arquitectónico completamente acristalado parece un escaparate gigantesco y, junto con la torre elíptica de cristal de 65 metros de altura marca la entrada oeste hacia el centro urbano.

BMW Welt

Coop Himmelb(l)au
Bollinger + Grohmann (SE)

2006
Georg-Brauchle-Ring
Schwabing

www.bmw-welt.com
www.coop-himmelblau.at

Flexibilität und Transparenz zeichnet den in Nähe des BMW-Werks und -Museums liegenden Entwurf aus. Das von Coop Himmelb(l)au entworfene Gebäude ist eine große, durchlässige Halle mit unterschiedlichen, ineinander übergehenden Ebenen. Unverwechselbares Zeichen wird die skulpturenhafte Form des Daches sein.

The building design that is located near the BMW plant and museum is characterized by flexibility and transparency. The building design by Coop Himmelb(l)au is a large, accessible hall with different levels that merge into each other. The sculptural-style form of the roof will be an unmistakeable identifying feature.

La flexibilité et la transparence caractérisent le projet situé à proximité de l'usine et du musée BMW. Le bâtiment conçu par Coop Himmelb(l)au est un grand espace transparent formé de niveaux différents qui se rejoignent. Son caractère particulier est fourni par la forme sculpturale de son toit.

La flexibilidad y la transparencia caracterizan el proyecto situado en las cercanías de la fábrica y del museo de la BMW. El edificio proyectado por Coop Himmelb(l)au es una gran nave transparente con diferentes niveles que transitan los unos en los otros. La forma del techo a modo de escultura será el signo inconfundible.

Index Architects / Designers

Index Architects / Designers

Index Structural Engineers

Index Structural Engineers

Index Districts

Index Districts

Photo Credits

Name	Page
Averwerser, Jann	142, 143
Bachmann, Markus	112, 113
Beierle, Edward	82, 83
Betz, Oliver	36, 37, 38, 39
Buck, Marcus	140, 141
Erlacher, Gisela	78, 79
Esch, H.G.	42, 43, 60, 61, 180, 181
Frank, Peter	52, 53
Gagern, Franziska von	33
Graubner, Claus	174, 175
Hamm, Hubertus	30, 31, 44, 45
Heinrich, Michael	16, 17, 68, 69, 92, 93, 168, 169
Henthorn, Derek	128, 129
Hinrichs, Johann	56, 57, 58, 59
Hoernisch, Andreas	80, 81
Holzherr, Florian	10, 11, 44, 45, 66, 67, 174, 175
Höpfner, John	58, 59
Hueber, Eduard	34, 35
Jakobsen, Katrin	146, 147
Jung, Oliver	172, 173
Katzer, Simon	50, 51
Kaunat, Angelo	22, 23
Kinold, Klaus	56, 57
Koyupinar, Haydar	63
Lelman, Mik	138, 139
Leppert, Quirin	132, 133
Lösch, Tommy	32
Matthäus, Eckhart	54, 55
Meyer, Robert	22, 23
Müller, Richie	86
Müller, Stefan	46, 47
Müller-Naumann, Stefan	32, 33, 64, 65, 72, 73, 89, 90, 91, 118, 119, 150, 151, 164,165, 176, 177
Myrzik + Jarisch	40, 41, 74, 75

Name	Page
Neudecker, Hans	56, 57
Palladium Photodesign	48, 49
Passoth, Jens	10, 11, 66
Pohlmann, Andreas	114, 115
Prokschi, Werner	144, 145
Pulfe, Wolfgang	136, 137
Riese, Karsten de	88
Rosenberg, Simone	66, 67, 82, 83, 122, 123
Schambeck / Schmitt	70, 71, 152, 153
Seyerlein und Seyerlein	14, 15
Soheli, Philipp	18, 19, 21
Steiner, Michael	102, 103
Viertelböck, Rainer	20
Waldmann	87
Weber, Jens	62, 84, 85, 178, 179
Wilhelmy, Dirk	96, 97,100, 101, 106, 107, 120, 121, 124, 125, 130, 131,134, 135, 158, 159, 160, 161, 162, 163, 170, 171
Zugmann, Gerald	76, 77

Other photographs courtesy

Allianz AG (148, 149), ArabellaSheraton (154, 155), Binnberg + Eberle Design + Architektur (24, 25), Boesel Benkert Hohberg Architekten (126, 127), Designreisen (166, 167), Fabien K (138, 139), Guggenbichler + Netzer Architekten (26, 27), Haberl Gastronomie (116, 117), High Light Business Towers (54, 55), Hotel Anna (98, 99), Hotel Cortiina (96, 97), Hotel Cosmopolitan (104, 105), Jürke Architekten (30, 31, 44, 45), Kempinski Hotel Airport München (108, 109), RPM Architekten (28, 29)

Imprint

Published by teNeues Publishing Group

teNeues Book Division
Kaistraße 18
40221 Düsseldorf, Germany
Phone: 0049-(0)211-99 45 97-0
Fax: 0049-(0)211-99 45 97-40
E-mail: books@teneues.de

Press department: arehn@teneues.de
Phone: 0049-(0)2152-916-202

teNeues Publishing Company
16 West 22nd Street
New York, N.Y. 10010, USA
Phone: 001-212-627-9090
Fax: 001-212-627-9511

teNeues Publishing UK Ltd.
P.O. Box 402
West Byfleet
KT14 7ZF, UK
Phone: 0044-1932-403 509
Fax: 0044-1932-403 514

teNeues France S.A.R.L.
4, rue de Valence
75005 Paris, France
Phone: 0033-1-55 76 62 05
Fax: 0033-1-55 76 64 19

www.teneues.com
ISBN 3-8327-9024-1

Bibliographic information published by Die Deutsche Bibliothek
Die Deutsche Bibliothek lists this publication in the Deutsche Nationalbibliografie;
detailed bibliographic data is available in the Internet at http://dnb.ddb.de

Editorial Project: fusion-publishing GmbH Stuttgart / Los Angeles
www.fusion-publishing.com
Edited and written by Joachim Fischer
Editorial coordination: Sabina Marreiros
Concept by Martin Nicholas Kunz
Layout: Thomas Hausberg
Imaging & Pre-press: Jan Hausberg
Maps: go4media. – Verlagsbüro, Stuttgart

Translation: SAW Communictions,
Dr. Sabine A. Werner,
Dr. Suzanne Kirkbright (English)
Sylvie Péjac (French)
Gemma Correa-Buján (Spanish)

Printed in Italy

14
15
7
22
81
63
62
3
65
24
64
19
30
45
32
27
20
12
80
18
67
Gabelsbergstraße
Brienner Straße
Barer Straße
26
25
Karolinenplatz
O.-v.-Millerring
Ludwigstraße
Hofga
55
Alter Botanischer Garten
Haupt-bahnhof
Residenz
73
74
71
48
70
49
57
29
72
54
31
43
59
50
58
42
23
Frauenkirche
2
Sonnenstraße
Theatinerstraße
Marien-platz
5
41
8
68
10
17
60
36
75
Viktualien-markt
61
51
44
76